Gerald Locklin

The Life Force Poems

Water Row Press
Sudbury
2002

The Life Force Poems. Copyright 2002 Gerald Locklin.

No part of this book may be reproduced, stored in a retrieval system, or transmitted in any form or by any means, electronic, mechanical, photocopying, recording, or otherwise, without the prior written permission of the copyright owner.

Grateful acknowledgment is given to the editors and publishers of all the periodicals and books in which some of this material has previously been published.

Water Row Press
PO Box 438
Sudbury MA 01776
email waterrow@aol.com
www.waterrowbooks.com
write for free catalogue

ISBN 0-934953-75-9 paper

Printed in USA
Cover illustration by Bruce Hilvitz.
Book design and typesetting by Henri Hadida.

Library of Congress Cataloging-in-Publication Data

Locklin, Gerald.
    The Life Force Poems: stories / by Gerald Locklin
        p. cm.
    ISBN 0-934953-75-9 (pbk.)
    I. Title.

PS3562.O265 L63 2001
811'.54--dc21

2001055931

DEDICATION

This book is dedicated to:

    Jeffrey Weinberg
    Joseph and Barbara Cowles
    Mat Gleason
    Patricia and Dave Cherin
    Tom Callinan
    Ron Burras
    Norman and Zelda Friedman
    Lou Boyles
    Tyler Dilts
    Jim and Eleanor Watson-Gove
    and all my wives, children and grandchildren

A number of the poems in this book were inspired by E.O. Wilson's <u>Consilience</u> and by the novels of A.S. Byatt.

CREDITS

Grateful acknowledgement is made to the following magazines and presses who previously published many of these poems, with sincere apologies to any who have been inadvertently omitted:

Ambit (London), The Reater, Tears in the Fence (Dorset), Coagula Art Journal, 5AM, Poetry International, Zerx Press, Nerve Cowboy, Slipstream, Bender, Free Thought, Lummox Journal, Lummox Press, Pariah Press / Heel Tap Magazine, Angelflesh, First Class, Baker Street Irregulars / Minotaur Press, Sheila-na-gig, Sundog, Home Planet News, New Laurel Review, One Dog Press, Spring: the Journal of the E.E. Cummings Society, Cider Press Review, Genre, Rising, Spillway, Cerberus, Staplegun, Rattle, Ragged Edge, Stovepipe, and The Wormwood Review.

The Life Force Poems

CONTENTS

I. Van Gogh's Van Gogh's 9

II. Intoxication 43

III. The Force 85

IV. Art and Life...125

V. Happiness 145

The Life Force Poems

I. **VAN GOGH'S VAN GOGH'S**

The Life Force Poems

HIS SANITY

of the seventy paintings
in this exhibition, perhaps
five are famous. it's the
others that strike one most,
in their simple painterly skill,
their originality of subject and treatment,
most of all in their lack
of "madness."

the thinness, for instance, of the
brushstrokes delineating a flowerpot
of chives. i don't remember
ever viewing a pot of chives
before. i joke to my wife that
he must have created them to
sprinkle on the ubiquitous
potatoes: baked? you know
that dairy cows will turn
up (turnip?) to provide
the sour cream.

trust me: this is a very
well painted pot of chives,
a million dollar pot of
chives, a pot of chives
you wouldn't be bored with
on your wall, a pot of
chives more endearing, in
certain ordinary ways, than, say,
a pot of electric irises,

an eminently sane pot of chives,

and yet far more than
merely competently rendered.

RED

and yet if it's an
intimation of insanity you're
looking for, a presage of
eventual suicide, i would
direct you to the redness
of the hair and beard, its
spikiness, the thin-skinned
redness of complexion. i bet
every elementary school teacher's
had a kid who looked like this
and couldn't sit still except for,
maybe, drawings, or music,
or perhaps was only happy on
the playing field. and at those
moments of an aptitude indulged,
complete absorption ruled. do i
mean every dane with red hair
is a lunatic, perhaps the whole
of scandinavia and ireland
potential candidates for preventive
detention? no, of course not,
there are degrees of everything, and
emphases, genetic combinations,
nurture, nurture, nurture
modifying
nature, nature, nature.

but everyone who's sensitive to such

The Life Force Poems

signs and with broad experience of
human types and individuals has
seen in our time vincent as a
child, has worried for him,
prayed that he would find
his outlet, rule, expression,
his success, his usefulness,
his place among his peers,
his circle of appreciative friends,
his mate,
his context of solution,
the channeling of his gift,
his "thing."

THE PORTRAITS OF SELVES

1.

he painted himself so often
and yet he always looks
a little different,
he's always vincent, but
he's never quite the same.

the comfort of a soft felt hat -
it makes you want one of your
own, and is a contrast to
the scythes of hair.

2. THE PIPE

one of the simple pleasures
for a man who would know
little of the sexual in his life.
and the more urbane adult self-image:
feeling good about oneself, for once
a moment of relaxation. no one
leads a life of unrelieved intensity,
not very long, at least, not
thirty-seven years of it, not,
for instance, a life without sleep.
a curl of smoke, the gently
glowing embers of tobacco, a
sampling of earth's bounty, quiet
moment of good fellowship.

3. THE STRAW HAT

vincent as hick,
as bumpkin,
as (can you believe
it?) the sunday amateur,
in shock, with palette.

4.

sometimes in coat and collar,
bow-tie,
suitably attired for society,
almost debonair,

The Life Force Poems

a thinner face,
the need to sell a painting,
desire for acceptance,
tired of always being on
the outside looking in,
and thus conservatively dressed
as if to say,

"look at me:
i'm a serious artist.
i can move among you.
i can give you paintings
that you'll like,
if you will meet me half-way,
try to understand
what i'm attempting,
dare to look with the eyes
of tomorrow, not yesterday.

damn you, *look at me*:
i'm dressed for success;
i don't want to frighten you;
i'll give you something that you'll like-
what would you like-
i'll try;
i'll do my best;
i mean to please.

just *look at me*:
i'm a *parisian*,
honest.
i am *one of you*,
i'm *not*,
for christ's sake,
oscar wilde
or dennis rodman."

5. THE LEFTY

he holds his brushes
in his right hand,
balances his palette
on his forearm.

my wife points out
he was left-handed,
thus the angle at which
he faces his face.

i tell her of the reputation
of left-handed hurlers in baseball,
always playing with a different deck,
planetary cowboys,
residents of the thirteenth floor.

6. SELF-PORTRAIT AS AN ARTIST, 1887-1888

it's too late now.
i am no longer one of you.
i have failed to see the world
with your eyes.
you have failed to see
what i see.

swedenborg understood *aura*.
i am trapped within mine now,
and reconciled to
my visionary prison.

The Life Force Poems

i am lost to your world,
i am no more anything but artist.

ALMOND BLOSSOM

if you don't look closely at
the rings of the branches,
it could be by anyone.
well, anyone who was among
the greatest painters of the
century: matisse, perhaps.
anyone who had studied
prints from the japanese.
anyone who loved light,
and living things.
anyone who believed in
the rebirth of nature,
the seasons of existence,
the blossoming of the creative.

anyone who had
absorbed the centuries,
had mastered his techniques
and from whose eyes
the scales had fallen.

VAN GOGH DIED CHILDLESS

and it troubled him that his brother, theo, named
a son <u>vincent</u>. you can
read about it in <u>still life</u>,
a novel by antonia byatt,

a book you should read anyway.

he seemed to find it
a distraction,
a needless extra pressure on him,
an anomaly he did not want
or need.

the sociobiologists see no need
to explain the egotism of the
human: they take it as a given,
the force
that drives us to adapt,
survive, and procreate, to
keep alive "the selfish gene."
it's <u>altruism</u> needs explaining.

sometimes it takes the face of
devoting oneself to the children
of others, a sister's perhaps,
as my childless aunt pat
devoted her life to me,
and now i am the one
who has the children
and the grandchildren.

it can be the firemen,
the soldiers, or the
anonymous citizen hero
who lays down his
life to save that
of another.

the mother who dies in childbirth,
the medical researcher,
the schoolmarm,

The Life Force Poems

the priest,
mother theresa,
the pope whom millions of the
poor, the faithful, call out
to as <u>papa</u>,
father.

it can also be the artist,
giving all to his art.

van gogh died childless,
but his suns and cypresses and irises
today
make us want to live,
intensely,
and to give life,
share it,
propagate it like
a field of grain.

so young i wrote of him,
an unpublished "starry night,"
of course,
about as bad as jim croce's.
i have been more alive
because of him--
we all have.

i am an animal;
we all are;
so was he.

but art lives also,
in a life my dog
in the backyard
does not get to enjoy,

although he loves his food,
and exercise,
and praises,
as much as i do.

i have my son with me today,
he too an artist.

van gogh did not die childless.

THE SHOES

he painted a <u>pair of clogs</u>
and, later, a <u>pair of leather shoes</u>.
have you ever tried to function
in a pair of shoes that didn't fit?
do you know the terminal blisters
you can develop playing, say, basketball,
or tennis, or football,
any sport that demands
radical stops and starts,
friction of skin against floor,
field, or canvas, wearing
inadequate footwear.
do you know what nikes mean
to a kid in the ghetto,
or boots to an infantryman?

as a kid i knew incredible pain
from layers of blisters and calluses,
the legacy of an obsession with sports.
my father had an ointment he rubbed
on my feet at bedtime, and it worked,
i don't know what it was.

The Life Force Poems

i wish i still had some.

my mother would get angry
when i'd be in too great discomfort,
after practice,
to enjoy eating out at a restaurant with her.
i'd spoiled her day. it seemed that
in such unintended ways,
i was always spoiling
her overcrowded, overly ambitious days.

when i tried to play football
with the big boys
on a scholarship at holy cross,
the trainers gave me a
hardened pair of cleats,
too small, and the blisters
were soon so bloody and sore that
i lost the little quickness
might have saved me.

today with vascular problems,
i wear birkenstocks, an
aid against edema.
and, when i walk the dog,
a loosely laced pair of
cheap running shoes, that
are falling apart at the seams.
i need to splurge on a new
pair at the discount store.
i forgot to bring them with me
to the gym a few weeks ago
and after an hour on the treadmill
developed a strained knee and -
the eternal woe of the aging -
it still hasn't gone away.

so, value your comfortable shoes-
softened, roomy, molded
to your contours, your routines,
your leather aura,
and value van gogh
who valued the peasant,
the laborers,
that we do not cease to be.

MONTMARTRE

i wish i'd been alive
when it was still a butte
of vegetable gardens, ramshackle
sheds, and functioning windmills
above the moulin rouge, when
agriculture was still a part of
the urban, when the peasant
lived not far from the factory
worker, or was the same person.

but i'm a creature of nostalgia,
regretful that i arrived in southern
california after the days of
film noir, the real hollywood,
although there was still a lot of
wasteland between l.a. and long
beach in 1964, and dairy valley
wasn't yet cerritos, and citrus
groves still lined the boulevards
of orange county, and the strawberry
fields had not given way to the
corporate headquarters of mitsubishi,
hyundai and toyota.

and could the light of
paris really be that bluer,
airier, than in the lowlands?
or are we talking atmosphere,
the expanding horizon of the
artist, the seeming escape
from the provinces, the
parochial, the impoverishment, to
the gaiety of the capital
of the art world, the
cabarets, the centuries of
inspiration and accomplishment.

light or lightheadedness or a
light heart and a lightened burden,
all, no doubt, all: and the
unbearable lightness of being
young.

GLASS OF ABSINTHE AND A CARAFE

that's a very large glass of
absinthe. no doubt
already diluted with the
water from the carafe. the
comparative volumes are
appropriate, as are the only
slightly contrasting colors.

still, i never drank that
large a glass of pernod,
never drank absinthe at
all. the opportunity might

tempt me briefly off the
wagon. it wouldn't
kill me on the spot or
send me on a rampage.

and always one sees the passing
life of the city through
the unremarkable rectangular window
of the cafe's winter partition,
just as hemingway did, a tyro from
oak park, penning three of the
greatest stories of our century in
a simple morning in the closerie des lilas
and celebrating with
a lunch of shellfish and white wine.

THE ÎLE GRANDE JATTE

how have i managed to miss it?
probably i passed beneath the
bridge glassed in a bateau mouche
with my dozing children,
didn't catch the announcement
in french from the crackling speaker.
maybe they didn't bother to announce
it out of the tourist season.

seurat, van gogh, sondheim,
for starters. i guess today it's
condos anyway, and the
seine a lot like the l.a. river,
channeled in concrete for flood control,
not life-sustaining water bordered
by banks of vegetation, ducks and geese,

The Life Force Poems

the leaves of autumn changing colors
on the ordinary trees. the
insignificance of the individual
is no longer even a theme,
just taken for granted now.

THE YELLOW HOUSE

build a yellow house
and they will come.

a yellow building, actually.

but in fact they don't come.

or they come - gauguin at least -
and leave.

even with the broad street
and a restaurant around the corner.

even with the sky a deeper
blue than the mediterranean.

even after you've painted the
shutters a sherwood green.

even with the fine tile roofs
to match the summer trees.

even with white awnings and
white-bonneted neighbors,

you wait , week after week,

in your warm yellow house
and no one comes
(or gauguin comes and goes)
until, at last, only
sorrow comes to your door.

SKULL WITH A SKELETON WITH BURNING CIGARETTE

studying at the art academy
in antwerp, van gogh wrote his
brother that his fellow students
were learning to draw <u>correctly</u>,
but that their works were <u>dead</u>.

so he painted an oil of the <u>dead</u>
that was both <u>correct and alive</u>.

proving there is nothing wrong with
distinguished study if you do not
allow it to erode your independence
and fidelity to what you've learned
first hand (doing a bit of poetry
editing, i find the most interesting
work arriving from the relatively
young who have combined the technical
lessons of creative writing classes
with experience that preceded study.
add: irreverence. add: indomitability.)

proving that even the deadly serious
can retain a sense of humor.

The Life Force Poems

SMOKING SKULLS II

the skull is enjoying its cigarette.
it looks downright happy.

could heaven consist of
untaxed vices

that can't kill you twice?

THE COURTESAN, 1887

the print by keisai eisen
that served as a model
is of a woman a trifle
long of face, but youthful,
feminine, seductively suggestive
of both innocence and skill.

van gogh enormously elaborated
color, detail, and context,
but his woman is enough to
scare you back into your
jockey shorts. you'd be
better off fucking the
frog on the lily-pad
at her feet. this face
could launch infinite volleys
of smack-talk: "yo' mama
modeled for van gogh!"
her hair-do resembles
a bag-pipe medusa and
she seems to suffer from

facial scoliosis.

somehow, i don't think the former
protestant divinity student was
truly in tune with oriental
eroticism. he's turned sex
into a mocking death mask,
a caricature of lust,
a comic book memento mori.

on the other hand, most
whores are not beautiful,
and they do transmit diseases.

in our age, vincent could have
made a good living drawing
pictures to discourage us from
unprotected sex, or
any sex at all.

A PETAL

the inspiration of his early years
was jean-françois millet. in elementary
school we studied edwin markham's
the man with the hoe, based on
millet's angelus, peasants pausing
in the fields from the labor that
has slanted their brows, eroded
their aspirations, rendered their
coloration earth-toned. and yet, a
dignity, indeed a spirituality, glows
unextinguished within the clods of
dirt that life conspires to

The Life Force Poems

turn them into.

the peasants at their humble
communion in <u>the potato eaters</u>
have the snouts of pigs, the
muzzles of dogs, the
brows of painters. you wonder
whether vincent, despite his human
sympathy, had bought into some
pseudo-darwinian quackeries of
physiognomy, a phrenology of
the face, the poor not turned by
labor closer to the beast of
burden, but almost animals at birth.

still, he himself was not bad-
looking, and, from this
family, emerges one almost pretty
female face, like one of the petals
on the "wet, black, bough"
of ezra pound's crowd in the
metro station, urban,
proletariat counterparts of
the peasantry. beauty survives,
beauty emerges and, even
genetically, beauty will prevail.

CRAB ON ITS BACK

the catalogue views it as a
highly skillful still life, praising
brushwork and rendering of
"concavities" and drawing a possible
connection between the vulnerability

of the upended crustacean and that
of van gogh after driving gauguin
from arles. certain adjectives, however
do suggest the sexual:
"aggressively volumetric" (whatever
that means) and "hot-tinted."

to me the crab is clearly
a woman on her back, more
threatening than vulnerable, with
vagina boldly foregrounded.

i have no idea what this
might say of van gogh,
or about
(thank you, dr. rorschacht)
me.

THE SEA AT LES SAINTES-MARIES-DE-LA-MER, JUNE, 1888

when i think of him i don't
think of the sea, as easy as it
might have been for him (or us) to
find a soulmate in its turmoil
and its depths.

no, he seems to have been mainly
challenged by the astonishing unpredictability
and shifts of its colors, and
those of the sky above it. to
theo he wrote of the mediterranean's
"mackerel" hues--a term we generally
give to skies--and notes transformations
of violet, green, blue, pink, gray. we might

ourselves find patches of gold, bronze, umber.

his concern, in other words, was not with
rendering his inner life as the sea,

but in getting the sea as itself,
in being true, in a static medium,
to the dynamic truth of its color.
he was not the madman/artist here:
simply the artist,
and his art was
for the sake of art.

FISHING BOATS ON THE BEACH AT SAINTES-MARIES-DE-LA-MER, JUNE, 1888

their masts as leafless twigs.
the sky a dome of light and wet.
boats beached and afloat.
the tide invading and retreating,
an eternal tease.

the boats' relations to each other:
angles, depths, dimensions,
weathered reds and whites and greens
and blues and blacks.

transition of brown sand
to burnt but lighter grasses.

he sketched the boats
in an hour, effortlessly.

this comes at the end of

the artistic maturation process,
misunderstood by students,
critics, and the public.

not carelessness but experience.

old picasso, impossibly prolific,
unable _not_ to be creative.

easy? let's see _you_ do it.

genius? sure, but remember
the chestnut: "sir, could
you tell me how to get
to carnegie hall?"
"practice, practice, practice."

THE BOULEVARD DE CLICHY

what is the difference
between his boulevard
and those of caillebotte?

his is not grand, nor is
the focus on the fashionable.

his is less populated, and the
people aren't out for a stroll--
they're hurrying to get someplace.

his is a thoroughfare of
molecules in motion, of which the
pedestrians are only a part.

The Life Force Poems

he sees like the scientist,
not like the journalist.

mondrian will abstract,
in different cities,
from his verticality of structures,
his horizontal arteries.

the earth is encircled by winds,
even the urban concentrations,
warmed and cooled by them,
and counter to their turning.

the paris night belongs to
hemingway, toulouse-lautrec, my memories:
he painted mornings.

WHEAT FIELD, WHEAT FIELD WITH REAPERS, WHEAT FIELD WITH CROWS

too much activity overtaxes the circuits.
too much life can kill.
beneath surfaces lie seizures.
paths lead everywhere and nowhere.
crows come to us from the beyond;
we do not scare them.
do they scare us?
do they fly in our faces
like those of da vinci and freud?

can paints be lathered on
in such thick layers
as to stand out from
the page of a portfolio,

stubby brushstrokes we can touch,
and in so doing
touch the painter across even
time and death?

the sun is blue and blackening,
but unextinguished in
the golden void of night.

STILL LIFE WITH BIBLE, AND STILL LIFE WITH BOOKS

they say that great writers
are great readers. the same
may be said of many painters.

these books are dogeared, faded,
frayed, read and re-read.

zola and goncourt: the
urban naturalists. the world
as a laboratory experiment--
character formed by heredity
and environment. the latter
predominating in democratic
america, "blood" of more
importance to the europeans.

and now, even in america, the
pendulum of influence has swung
back to genetic research, genetic
predisposition to everything from
addictions to altruism.
in a cultural context, and
with caution against racism

The Life Force Poems

and lack of compassion, but
beginning to cut through the
mist of pop psychology and
sociology and deconstructive
politics. thus, the portraiture
of the poor: the potato
eaters, the barmaid, the
prostitute, the woman sewing
and winding yarn, the
old woman from arles, the one-
eyed man, the repeated self-
portraits: what past lives on
in me? who am i now? where
can i possibly aspire to travel?
what must i channel or do
battle with all of my life?

and the more balzacian bourgeoisie: what
is the mystery of their
domesticity, success in commerce.
the owner of a restaurant, the
exotic zouave. his crowning/joy:
to have captured portraits
of an entire family that had
adopted him into their sympathies:
the postman/revolutionary, joseph
roulin of arles, his wife
augustine, his little boy,
his baby girl.

he said portraiture brought him
closest to "the infinite" and was
"the only thing in painting"
moved him "to the depths."

his science was the felt

truth of the human, the
intuition of the evolutionary
mystery, the biochemistry
that constitutes our brilliance
and our suffering, that keeps
our bedroom always slightly
out of kilter, lacking
in perspective, dizzying, that
animates our lives and brings
us to our blazing or
eroded deaths.

VEGETABLE LOVE

he sired no children, yet
celebrated, like monet, the
lush fertility of spring and summer:
<u>trees and undergrowth</u>, <u>a park
in spring</u>, <u>daubigny's garden</u>,
<u>wheatfields</u>, <u>harvests</u>, <u>blossoms</u>
and, significantly, <u>courting couples
in the voyer d'argenson park
at asnières</u>. to sustain the
ordinary, the common, the essential,
and to validate it, some must
sacrifice it from their expectations.

STILL LIFE WITH BIBLE

vincent juxtaposes his father's
monumental bible with zola's
<u>joie de vivre</u>.

The Life Force Poems

i never thought of zola
as a helium balloon, but
i suppose that, contrasted
with job and jeremiah, he
might qualify as, if not
a bushel of laughs, at
least a barrel of monkeys.

THE COTTAGE

little more than
a mud hut on the muddy flats
for those who labor on the soil
and gradually sink into it,
become it, the skies at end
of day as earthen as their skins.

i remember the early evenings
of welsh winter, abolishing
the concept of an afternoon.
but we had a large and various
dinner to look forward to,
potatoes, yes, but also
butter, salt, and pepper,
lamb or pork chops, gravy,
turnips, spinach and brussels sprouts,
soup and salad,
english cheeses,
english biscuits,
french wines,
english beers.
in a centrally heated duplex,
with an almost american shower.
an evening of the b.b.c.,

Gerald Locklin

if we wanted,
or reading in a comfortable chair,
with more than adequate illumination.
an expensive sound system.
feather beds, a plump cat,
and the next door neighbors'
intelligent and loyal border collie.
a pub within walking distance,
for one last one, if it wasn't pouring.

no wonder my wife would love
to return to wales,
whereas vincent, having
ministered to the lowland
miners, left holland,
never to return.

THE VICARAGE AT NUENEN

to me it seems
a pleasant enough place,
solid and unimaginative,
but lots of windows,
ample attic,
warmly clothed neighbors, gossiping,
trees and hedges and
a glow, though sober, to the sky.

no more than upstate new york,
where fall was the most
colorful and lively season,
and religion was also
still taken seriously.
but i understand the

The Life Force Poems

parochialism and provincialism
that he fled from,
the paralysis of unambitious places,
the tyranny of the parental conscious,
the monotony of civic duty,
how we are held hostage by
the reciprocity due those who love us.
we all appreciate the warmth
of families our friends have left,
even as we are chilled by
what has transpired for
our friends who stayed at home.

i had the best of families,
as vincent did,
but it's unthinkable to me
not to have left,

and on those rare occasions
when i pay a return visit
i am gripped by fear
that i will never get away again:
why have i given this place
one more chance to capture me?
nostalgia passes,
i see all i need to see,
i use the place up in a day.
i can't wait for
the plane to leave the ground.

ROOFS IN PARIS

the rooftops of paris,
the sidewalks of paris,

Gerald Locklin

the cafes and businesses of paris,
the churches of paris,
the three hills of paris,
the windmills of paris,
the boulevards of paris,
the cobblestones of paris,
the parks of paris,
the bridges over the seine,
the cemeteries of paris,
<u>les</u> <u>places</u> of paris,
the theatres of paris,
the prostitutes of paris,
the market-streets of paris,
the schools of paris,
the accordians of paris,
the museums of paris,
the race-tracks of paris,
the hotels, grand and small, of paris,
the thieves of paris,
the quais of paris,
the fishermen of paris,
the fly-boats of paris,
the bookstores of paris,
the fashions of paris,
the breakfasts of paris,
the schoolgirls of paris,
the old ones of paris,
the lovers of paris . . .

I could go on . . .

paris exists to be painted
and as
a setting for the unforgettable,
the indelible.
paris exists so that

The Life Force Poems

we may die, knowing that
we have lived.
paris is everything
that disneyland can never be.
paris does not want
to be some other place.
paris is first.
paris, even with mcdonald's,
is itself.
paris is paris.
paris is not
in nevada.

The Life Force Poems

II. INTOXICATION

The Life Force Poems

INTOXICATION

1.

in an interview, my former student,
dave alvin, now justly admired as a
writer, singer, and player of songs,
takes note of my recent jazz poems:
"i know," he says, "that you've quit
drinking—do you think that music now
is filling the place that drinking
once did in your life?"

he's absolutely right, of course.
i'd be brought up breathless
by the astuteness of his insight if
i didn't already hold him in such high
esteem. i tell him that i was reflecting
on this very phenomenon, riding back a
week before from listening to danilo
perez and his trio at "the bakery":
the intensifying of the emotions that
scott fitzgerald attributed to alcohol,
the relinquishing of cares and motivation
in the dreamlike, womblike, death-enhancing
dance of the sinews, the relaxation into
pleasure that we once knew--<u>sometime</u>--
after a few gin-and-tonics.
yes, intoxication without side-effects,
without the hangovers.
intoxication stimulating creativity,
not superseding it.
intoxication that <u>enforces</u> memory,
that does not depress,

Gerald Locklin

that makes you want life
(or the moment)
not to end,
yet readies you for death.

yes, this is what i have these days
instead of stupor.

2.

baudelaire said, "be drunk always,
with wine, poetry, or virtue—
but be drunk always."

i take virtue to be rooted
in the latin <u>virtus</u>, strength.
thus, athleticism also
is intoxication. so too purity,
passion, and the sacrifice for
family or fellow man.

the warrior as well as oscar wilde.
pater and newman equally.
hopkins, hardy, housman.
nun, mother, matador, torch-singer.
all our enthusiasms subsumed into
the aesthetic, even the theology
and umbrage of a hightoned lady.

as for vino well, as the
archetypal bartender queries:
"what's your poison?"

mine, for now, is comprised of
the arpeggios, glissandos, pounding

The Life Force Poems

chords and chilling scales of this
piano player's central avenue,
panama and every place you've ever been
(i hear tangiers, havana, and macao;
bombay and the blue note;
east l.a. and south of the thames,

nile, amazon, and mississippi,

the river of humanity.

3.

paul klee's <u>rausch</u>,
<u>intoxication</u>,

is painted on burlap,
dated 1939.
the nazis had declared
his art degenerate,
his mind disordered.
the root is <u>toxic</u>.

and yet,
though red on brown and beige,
and roughly cut,
the sun and moon still occupy
at least a corner of the sky;
the animal is plump and,
though the head's detached,
it seems still to be smiling;
and man still has his eyes and
ears and nose and mouth.
maybe a monk, but with bangs.

is that a butcher's blade?

scaping or escaping the goat?

a man is blood and brain,
voice, hands, and belly.

klee left the "fatherland"
(sacrilegiously so-called)
for Switzerland
and died, in 1940,
in bern,
his birthplace,
as we all do.

NO LONGER A TEENAGER

my daughter, who turns twenty tomorrow,
has become truly independent.
she doesn't need her father to help her
deal with the bureaucracies of schools,
hmo's, insurance, the dmv.
she is quite capable of handling
landlords, bosses, and auto repair shops.
also boyfriends and roommates.
and her mother.

frankly it's been a big relief.
the teenage years were often stressful.
sometimes, though, i feel a little useless.

but when she drove down from northern California
to visit us for a couple of days,
she came through the door with the

The Life Force Poems

biggest, warmest hug in the world for me.
and when we all went out for lunch,
she said, affecting a little girl's voice,
"i'm going to sit next to my daddy,"
and she did, and slid over close to me
so i could put my arm around her shoulder
until the food arrived.

i've been keeping busy since she's been gone,
mainly with my teaching and writing,
a little travel connected with both,
but i realized now how long it had been
since i had felt deep emotion.

when she left i said, simply,
"i love you,"
and she replied, quietly,
"i love you too."
you know it isn't always easy for
a twenty-year-old to say that;
it isn't always easy for a father.

literature and opera are full of
characters who die for love:
i stay alive for her.

CLOSING THE BOOK

my last aunt died this fall,
at 94 or so (hers was a generation
that still valued privacy), and it
seems strange not to be lifting the
phone every couple of weeks to check
in with her, that i'm fine except

for minor aches and pains, inquire how
she is herself getting on, what with
her stubborn cataracts and club toe,
back in her apartment in upstate new
york where she lived for what? sixty
or seventy years? it's also sinking in
that the last source of family history
is gone—not that i ever really grilled
her anyway--i'd been trained as a child
that one does not pry -- and our secrets
were pitifully tame by today's standards
anyway. but the few things that i might
have asked her will go unbroached now--
like what enraged my eldest aunt,
elizabeth (the matriarch though not a
mother) to actually drive my mother from
the house of my aunts and uncles with a
broom one wintry rught during world war two,
when my father was away in the navy and
i was still young enough, maybe three, that
my mother tugged me home to our apartment
on a sled. it needn't have been a mortal
sin: maybe my mother had just
"given her some lip,"
or gone out for a drink or a movie
with one of my father's friends,
or worn an immodest dress -- by wartime
catholic standards -- or questioned the
authority of the clergy. it didn't take
much to be scandalous in those days -- and,
as we see in <u>dancing at lughnasa</u> --
respectability was often all an irish family
had to sustain its pride, its courage to go on.
i remember being virtually disowned for
disobeying and going to a bob hope film that the
legion of decency had rated "B"--

The Life Force Poems

not even the excommunicating "C" for
Condemned -- but gravely proscribed as a
danger to the faith and morals of the laity.

probably my last aunt wouldn't have
been privy to that battle anyway -- she
was married, so not living with her siblings.
probably it was just a matter of my mother,
a schoolteacher, asserting a bit of independence
in some small, symbolic way (she did have big
fights with my father when he got back from
the south pacific, though -- he storming out,
she weeping with a sister by the window.
those emotional donnybrooks ended when my
father was diagnosed with diabetes, the
level of hostilities reduced to petty
sniping and largely separate lives,
a lot like, come to think of it,
my own wife and myself.

no, i'm sure my late aunt wouldn't have
enlightened me as to what sparked the
flailing with the broom, even if she knew,
remembered, and i don't think it had some
big, symbolic, traumatic influence on my life.
all i recall are flashes of the straw,
the cupboard, my mother's arms raised
to ward off the blows, the icy sled-ride
with a scarf around my face.
it all seems vividly but distantly cinematic,
a scene fran a technicolor movie
of a dostoevski novel.

no doubt it all came down to birth order:
the eldest and the youngest of the fourteen
siblings clashing, authority and the rebel,

51

darwinian conservative and radical,
promethean, planetary,
but resolved by sunday dinner.

still, notice the combatants were women.
i've never bought that women before 1970
were powerless: my childhood simply contradicts that.
and now the past is buried, once and for all.
safe from my literary exposure.
and i am free to move,
in my own time,
from history to myth.

PAUL KLEE: ARCHANGEL

features sketched from pipes
and plumblines, the musical
scale and a spade,

from crook or hook or cane,
mitre or crozier,
bulb and flute:

against a background
of patches of pastels.

he doesn't seem to take
himself too seriously.
just stern enough to scare
the naughty kids when necessary.

an anthropomorphic angel,
but so what?

surfaces and substance

The Life Force Poems

are separate.

1938. he watches, bides his time.
in seven years his peer will plummet,
a short reich for the overreacher.
the hangman hangs himself.
let him have as much rope
as he wants, on credit.
the hit man is always his own
last assignment. then he who
would be god must hope
there isn't any.

PAUL KLEE: LITTLE ROOM IN VENICE

i never wear bright colors,
and i've never been to venice.
in the movies it is nearly
always sinister. hemingway
enjoyed it, but he was in
love and spent a lot of
time in harry's. also, i
suspect you get a better
table if you're hemingway.
i suppose the chamber of
commerce prefers <u>his</u> rendering
of their burg to that of, say,
thomas mann. i doubt that
either of them stayed
in little rooms.

i <u>always</u> seem to, though.
it just may be because i'm cheap.

i keep waiting for my
<u>europe on five dollars a day</u> book
to return to currency.

i might be happy in this
<u>blue</u> room, though. where even
the air is blue. and any
reds are filtered through the
blue to shades of pink. where
the window is a face with sun
and moon for eyes. the drapes a
bonnet. the windowsill a mouth. a
carpet doubling as a lawn.
a cross that's not a crucifix.
a clock set for sunset.

1933.
hitler's arrogation of authority.
mussolini preceded him, but venice
may have seemed a safer home.

at the end of the decade,
joyce, virginia woolf, and klee
had had enough.

HOORAY FOR KURT VONNEGUT

i am only on page 6 of <u>timequake</u>
and i am already writing my second poem
inspired by the book.
frankly, i could also have written poems
inspired by the other four pages
and by each page of the prologue.

The Life Force Poems

maybe more than one per page.

but this time i am writing because
kilgore trout just said,
"hooray for firemen."
i'll second that.
i have a son who's a fireman
and i'm very proud of him.
i'd be proud of him anyway--
he's the best son anyone could ask for,
as are my other two sons--
but i'm additionally proud that he set out
to become a fireman,
and he achieved it,
and he's a damn good one.

so i too say, hooray for firemen.
and i say hooray for kurt vonnegut
for always reminding us
of the simple, deep, abiding truths,
and of what a great spoken language--
or what great spoken languages--
we americans have evolved.

TELL ME ABOUT IT, PAL

i say to my son over spaghetti,
"my god, this semester has gone fast.
each one seems to go by even quicker."

and he says,
"yeah, it's like when your life is
almost over and you say to yourself,
'where did it all go?' and
'what am i going to do with all that

i've learned and no time to use it?"'

he's only a senior in high school.
how does he know these things so young?

he knows them because
already he's a writer.

DECISIONS, DECISIONS

this week's issue of esquire
is devoted to immortality,
how within five or ten years
the scientists may be able to

keep us alive forever,
if we so desire.

as if i don't have enough
to worry about already.

RUTH SCHÄCHTEROVÁ: PAYSAGE AVEC TROIS MAISONS

the three houses have three chimneys.
well, they are not really houses--
they are more like school buildings
or factory plants.
barracks maybe.

is that a swan or a snake?

The Life Force Poems

the rays of the sun
are spokes of a gear.

rectangles, rulers, scraps of
official documents.

the work is not that of a
mature artist trying to
affect the mind of a child:

it is, in fact, the art of a
young girl who was to be
dead at the age of fourteen,

and the landscape with three houses
is her village,
a concentration camp.

i found this in an essay
by milan kundera
in the <u>new yorker</u>,
reviewing a french exhibition
of the art produced by
prisoners of theresienstadt.
kundera discusses the centrality
of art to the human experience
and suggests that it is as important
that we remeber schönberg, kafka,
wittgenstein -- all the "decadent"
european jews of the twentieth century --
as that we remember hitler.

i used to eschew the "bookish,"
the "artist" in my poetry.
i used to write largely from

direct personal experience, and,
to an extent, i still do.
but i also find now,
in works of art, music, literature,
a triangulation of my own experience
as a child of the twentieth century.
and i celebrate the creations of
other children of our century,
of this millenium which humanity
and art somehow survived,
the works of our brothers and sisters
in the flesh, such as milan kundera
and this little girl.

ELIE NADELMAN: TANGO, 1919

1.

it's all the rage now
in the geriatric circles
and in foreign movies,
cinematographic choreography,
choreographed cinematography,
sex and symmetry,
the symmetry of simulated sex,

the mating dance
and ethnic matrix,

history and instinct
intertwined in the escape
from the quotidian into
the sensual.

The Life Force Poems

2.

but for these two,
the woman slightly taller
than the man,
wasp-waisted, thin of leg,
and bursting at the bosom,

both imperially attired,
newly coiffed,
and not quite touching,

it was formal as the minuet

(and yet, of course, a form of
foreplay, for them, and for the century.)

GEORGE BELLOWS: <u>PADDY FLANNIGAN</u>, 1908

bird-chested kid with bad teeth,
half-starved and spoiling for a fight,
he and his brothers wouldn't live long,
most of them,

but each succeeding generation
would be better off
in health, wealth, power,

up to a point.

Gerald Locklin

CHARLES SHEELER: <u>CLASSIC LANDSCAPE</u>, 1931

the smokestacks of the great american factories,
like an abstraction from palm trees
or windbreaking poplars,
presented a new man-made glory
against the panorama of the continental sky.
even the smoke seemed beautiful,
as smogsets still do sometimes.
how long did anyone live anyway?
who'd ever heard of pollution?
the need to win bread,
to bring home the bacon,
was a fact of life pre-empting emphysema.
starvation, malnutrition,
would kill you quicker than cancer.

thus, the slagheaps please as do
the smooth and crumpled dunes of
cape cod or the oregon beaches,
or the south dakota badlands.
silos, steamplants, pressurized cylinders
stand solid as the testament to progress.
the railroad tracks, as hart crane knew,
ran from and to the infinite.
the sky was not to be the limit.

i saw this in the boiler room
of the county penitentiary
where my father ran the giant generators,
but it scared me, left me joyless--
it was his world but not to be mine--
my aptitudes were those of

The Life Force Poems

my schoolteacher mother.

so, too, the vast facilities of eastman kodak,
bausch and lomb, ritter instruments--they
gave me no pleasure growing up in rochester,
nor did the using of the river and the lake
as sewer and cesspool.
i sought relief from the industrial
on the playing fields made possible
by corporate, paternalistic civic projects.
the local reformatory, incidentally,
was named "industry."

but i <u>was</u> exhilarated by my first experiences
of the southern California freeways,
the harbors of l.a. and long beach,
the city blocks of silent, windowless warehouses,
the twelve-throated power plant
on the alkali flats.
and i can respond to the
<u>vision</u> of a new aesthetic in this painting:
apotheosis of earth tones and the leaden paints.
a line as thin as aether separates
<u>ekstasis</u> from depression

with its many meanings.

PAUL STRAND: <u>WALL STREET</u>, 1915

the monolithic marble building,
with its opaque anti-windows,
a hundred feet high,
hearkens forward to the third reich

Gerald Locklin

and enclave institutions of
our current downtown business districts.

and it more than occupies
more than its share of the frame--
for all that we can see
it may go on for many blocks--
it may be almost all there is.

certainly it dwarfs
the workers and the wealthy
inadvertently parading up the sidewalk.
they cast long shadows in
the thin light of late afternoon.
the structure stops light dead.

in those days we were labor
exploited by capital;
today we all,
in one way or another,
own a piece of the market.
we are upwardly mobile,
though what goes up may come down.
certainly no one is free of it.
what you can't beat, consider joining.
some say there's got to be a better way.
it wasn't east germany.
i guess today it is
a kinder, gentler wall street
(i say with my fingers crossed).

still, no one lives there.

The Life Force Poems

EDGAR DÉGAS: COTTON MERCHANTS OF NEW ORLEANS, 1873

sink your hands into
the clouds of cotton.
paint your walls a white
that is only slightly creamier than
the white of cotton.
import africa for its
color-coded contrasts.
even the creoles, of course,
are less white than
the white of cotton.
eschew purity for revelry:
the white of cotton is purity enough.
set sail on the billowy seas
of cotton, not the soiled green of
the ocean framed upon the wall.
wear white shirts.
wear straw hats and top hats.
don't try to paint in the sunlight
which could blind a european.
or a brother's wife,
the model estelle.
consider the cotton candy.
dive into it like scrooge mc duck.
melville knew that madness
was the color of absence.
poe knew that madness was
the glare of the north pole.
now dégas, who would return from
a year among family, amidst a culture
of gumbo, jambalaya, spice, humidity,
and the erasure, in the sun, of

boundaries, to an art as exclusionary
as the colorlessness that denies itself:
always the observer -- of the dance,
the horses, the operatic ascension--
never the participant.

WILLEM DE KOONING: MONTAUK HIGHWAY, 1958

i like it.
i think i can see the sense is which
those broad, brown strokes
are the road itself, and represent
speed, rush, blur,
the man/machine in motion.

maybe i'm wrong.
what, for instance, about
that oblong of blue.
maybe it's a picture of
a bluebird in a wheat field,
or a memory of the ocean
when one has forgotten
having lived once at the sea.
maybe it's a homage to vincent
van gogh, whose paintings often
ended up as golden and azure as
day and night.

maybe it's just what
de kooning felt like
doing with his oils and
papers and canvas the day
that he did it.

or the blowsy night.

anyway, i like it.
i like to look at it.
it almost makes me want to drive
the montauk highway.
i'm afraid that once i got there, though
(it's three thousand miles away,
as the crow flies ((crookedly))), i'd
wonder what the fuck i was doing there.
i'd rather be back home here
looking at a picture in the newsletter
of a museum.

don't give it to me, either.
i don't want to have to
look at it constantly. i have
my own life, my own road, a
different one (though not entirely
of dissimilar hues).

i have my cat to feed.

A SIGHT I'D HATE TO SEE

when i hear academics speaking of
"presenting" at a conference,
i try to assume that
they haven't read
<u>the naked ape</u>.

JOHN SINGER SARGENT: ENA AND BETTY, DAUGHTERS OF ASHER AND MRS. WERTHEIMER

if you ever need an illustration
of the intersection of
heredity and sibling differentiation,

study these two ladies,
young and less young,
their contrasting faces,
shoulders, gowns, and gestures,

oh-so-similar, yet not the same.

JOHN SINGER SARGENT: THE DAUGHTER OF DARLEY BOIT, 1882

variously bemused
by the gaze of the portraitist,
they do not even look a lot alike.
even before our psychologic century,
the american girl,
of privilege at least,
is growing independent.
only the archetypal urns
they lean against in moments of distraction
stand taller than their personalities.

a foolish critic notes their "sexuality,"
but it is the antithesis of this,
their new-world innocence,
virgins of the virgin continent,

The Life Force Poems

that constitutes their childhood beauty
and will later render them more prized
than european women of greater sophistication,
fashion-plates of ostentatious sensualism.

(of course their daddy's virgin wealth
won't <u>hurt</u> their chances.)

the foregrounded youngest,
playing with her pinafored doll,
<u>is</u> the living doll of lyric commonplace.
the two teenagers,
clad in white on black,
rembrandt pale in fathomless shadow,
prefigure begrman's <u>persona</u>,
posed in perpendicularity,
the erect/the relaxed,
one ready for the world,
one fixed upon the self/same other.
in the light, miss confidence
puts one foot forward,
at balletic angle,
on the threshold of a slender, be-tressed perfection.

they do not think to read their destinies
in the mazes and spoked mandalas
of the epigenetic omar khayam carpet.

their freedom will consist of
their response to what life
has to offer them.
the rooms they occupy will cease to seem
quite as spacious as
the mansions of remembrance.
this is the tragedy and dignity

we cannot spare our little girls.

BUTTERFLY

there's an 86-year-old woman
who swims laps at the y.
she was once an olympic swimmer
in the backstroke,
and later was chair of an art department.
she still swims straight,
with remarkable mobility in her shoulders,
and, incidentally, glides considerably
faster than i do. she swims at least
half an hour a day, probably closer
to an hour.

the astonishing thing to me
is that she even swims the butterfly stroke.
that stroke is way beyond
both my coordination and my stamina
but when i mentioned to her once that,
at fifty-seven, i guessed i wouldn't
be mastering any new strokes,
she said, "oh don't be silly --
you're never too old to learn --
why i didn't teach myself
the butterfly
until i was in my late 60s."

The Life Force Poems

FORGET THE FINISHING LINE

my buddy stuart at the ymca
has recently, in his seventies,
added weightlifting to
his swimming and his golf
and paul, in his eighties,
still swims and golfs as well.
they're both still interesting guys
to talk to also,
not only about their pasts
but about sports, politics,
their kids and grandkids,
you name it.
they both enjoy a good laugh too.

i've always heard that
hanging out with the young
will keep you young yourself.
on the other hand, i've known guys
who caused themselves a lot of grief
by trying to pretend they were
hipper than they were.

so i'm not advocating
"acting your age,"
which can be a form of
group control of the individual --

i'm just suggesting that
it may also keep you young
associating with the youthfully old,
who are not embarrassed by their years

nor intimidated by them,
and who provide not only inspiration
but the added comfort of knowing
where you yourself are coming from
and what you may be going through.

LAVENDER MIST REVISITED

it's all there,

the surface and the strings,
deep breathing and held breath,
the x-ray and the cat-scan,
time and timelessness,
the forest and the trees,
perfume and vacuum,
the impenetrable wilderness of childhood.

god and darwin,
meaning and the void,
desire and the zero absolute.

after you have said such art,
you're free to die.

PAGLIACCI

the director, zeffirelli,
considers the clown
evil incarnate, redeemed
only slightly by his arias.

The Life Force Poems

he feels this aging actor
should have understood
a younger woman needs
a young man to have
children by, to raise
a family with.

the tenor, placido domingo,
sympathizes with his role.
he's loved the girl totally,
done everything for her.
yes, his sexuality is aggressive,
possessive, exclusive, but
such are the males who have
dominated the process of
natural selection--the
"new males" of feminist myth,
sympathetic, supportive, permissive
have been the evolutionary
losers.

is zeffirelli gay?

as in <u>carmen</u>,
we are confronted here
with tragic, genetic paradox:

violent passion,
obsessive and irritated,
preceding and subsuming
civilized conditioning,
yields death as well as birth,
survival of the strong yoked
to his self-destruction.

the tough and virile man grows old;

he too will wear his pantaloons rolled.

and then the comedy is finished.

VÉRISMO

their slices of life
are sure more heavily plotted
than any slices of mine.

HILLARY AND JACKIE

of course i loved the film:

i have had ample lifetime
to observe both sibling rivalry
and sibling loyalty,
competition and differentiation,
the force of birth order,
the shock and lifelong sadness
of dethronement.

i have known the love of sisters,
for each other
and by me.

i have known the love of london
and the love of wales.

i have loved concerti
of the cello,

The Life Force Poems

elgar, dvorac,
and the women
who play them.

of course i loved the film.

WHAT WE HAVE

like gerald haslam's story,
"that constant coyote,"
it's about ways society
prepares the individual for death.

in our time, we do not have
their ritual easings:

>	the sacrament of extreme unction,
>	the elysian fields,
>	the <u>ode: tintern abbey</u>
>	the ritual cohesion of chagall,
>	the ways of the navajo,
>	the songlines of the outback,
>	fern hill and llareggub.

we live on in our children, though,
and in our influence on those we've taught,
by eloquence, wit, or example.

WHEN YOU COME TO THE END OF A PERFECT DAY

you have,
thanks to dr. kevorkian,

self-assisted suicide
(and the encouragement
of beneficiaries).

DEATH WISH

brian garfield wrote the novel
as an attack on
vigilante justice.

naturally the movie,
and its sequels,
launched a cavalcade
of vigilantes.

the author went on t.v.
to plead against the influence
of what hollywood had wrought,
but to little avail.

i knew brian in graduate school
at the university of arizona,
as generous a spirit
as you'd ever want to meet,
and i retain a great respect for him.

but the episode symbolizes for me
how little liberals understand
the strength and history
of human nature.

The Life Force Poems

DECONSTRUCTION, DECENTERING, DEMYTHOLOGIZING

new words for
old lies.

CONNECT THE DOTTED LINES

<u>death in venice</u>,
<u>brief encounter</u>,
<u>last tango in paris</u>,
<u>rocky</u>:

these are all films
that would be virtually impossible
to turn off,
no matter how many times
you'd already seen them,

even if only on the basis of
the hypnotic magnetism of
their musical scores.

question: what themes do
they have in common?

STARTING POINT

it occurs to me
while walking with my wife and dog
along a dusty mountain road
why we worry about things

(don't you? i do.)
that we'll never live to see,
like the sun burning down
or the ocean drying up-

it's the selfish gene in us
that cares,
the one that wants to live
forever.

i tell my wife this,
and she says, "we care about
the world our kids and grandkids
and their kids will live in,
because we love them so."

and i agree,
but i suspect
that it's the selfish gene
that makes it possible
for us to love unselfishly.

FAMA FUGIT

there was a woman at the concert
looked exactly like an aging
lauren bacall.

of course lauren bacall is aging,

but what would it be like to go through life
looking like a movie star,
especially one with the class
and style and highly individual

The Life Force Poems

good looks of a lauren bacall?

to know you were as beautiful
as lauren bacall,
and yet not the original,
not the real thing,
even if you came first?

to know that you,
in contrast to lauren bacall,
were not famous,
not world-class in your field,
that beneath your uncanny resemblance
you were cursed with ordinariness,
with being forgotten even sooner
than lauren bacall will be.

THE GENE DOES NOT GO GENTLE

i used to feel that the themes
of dylan thomas's early poems,
that man is a poet of biology
and thus "the force that through
the green fuse drives the flower"
drives our "green age also,"

and that "death
shall have no dominion,"
because our molecules live on in
the earth and animals and stars

were a sort of easy and obvious
pantheism that was no more than
an excuse for the music

of the poems.

now i'm not sure that those aren't
(along with the childhood-as-eden
of the later works)
the theme that underlies all others.

TO BE AND BE AND BE

were shakespeare's children
equally important with
his plays?

it's possible that this is
what the plays
are saying.

it's also possible,
(and appropriately paradoxical)

that this is what
the comedies of
oscar wilde are saying
also.

THUS, THE MILLSTONE

freud's insistence that
even the child is sexual
was not a justification
for predation upon innocence

The Life Force Poems

but an early recognition that
we all live
to give life.

to inflict adult sexuality
upon a child
is to frustrate and pervert
the process of creation.

GRAY PANTHERS

why do you think they want
their kids to have kids?

do you think they really want
retirement jobs
as babysitters?

QUALITY OF LIFE OR LIFE ITSELF?

the supposedly advanced civilizations,
japan as well as europe and
white america,

are contracepting themselves right out
of hegemony, if not indeed existence.

norman mailer knew this
and thus was ridiculed,
just as he was for saying masturbation
was always second-rate sex.

and parents of all races,
it's time to butt out of
your children's sexual choices.

AN OCCASIONAL COYOTE

in the high ranch desert valley,
people are painting their houses
cape cod blue,
planting irrigated lawns,
fencing their yards,
and paving their driveways.

the wild burrows that used
to rut in the night
and dump their odorless vegetarian shit
to be cleansed by the endless wind,
have been rounded up,
thus effectively leaving the area
without remaining signs of wildlife.

the above have been accomplished
to make it more convenient
for city-dwellers to get
back to nature.

A PENNY FOR YOUR THOUGHTS

we all seem to want
to sum up our lives
in loosely bound works:
the meditations of marcus aurelius,

The Life Force Poems

<u>les pensées</u> of pascal,
the notebooks and essays
of emerson and thoreau,
<u>the gettysburg address</u>,
<u>the tower</u> and <u>crazy jane</u>
(not <u>a</u> <u>vision</u>;
not <u>a</u> <u>fable</u>):

even bukowski let himself
be talked into
<u>the captain is out to lunch</u>
<u>and the sailors have taken over the ship</u>,

and it didn't turn out
all that bad.

others tackle the task straight on,
like a linebacker who knows
he can't be steamrolled.
here i have in mind
beethoven's final string quartets,
<u>the four quartets</u> of t.s. eliot,
the <u>book of ecclesiastes</u>,
the <u>lives of christ</u>.

JACKSON POLLOCK: ONE: NUMBER 31, 1950

suddenly we realize that this is everything:
the universe, the self, the molecules,
their nuclei, motion, rest, the stars,
desire, shakespeare, color, absence, heat
and light, anxiety, the umbilical telephone,
the beast and beauty, chaos, order,
stimulus, perception, the creative,

virginia woolf, the waves, emotion,
monasteries, christ and shiva,
music, wagner, bach, miles, coltrane,
philip glass and seymour, dna,
the life of the senses,
the life of the mind,
life, literature, lifelessness,
death, time, eternity,
the teapot in the tempest,
control and spontaneity,
space, boundlessness, boundaries,
you name it.

it's all here.
all language.
all there is to see.
all there is to hear.
all there is to think.

sleep never stops.

THE MOTIVE

as a writer you get to seek
popularity or immortality,
riches or fame,
rewards for your labor
in this life or the next.

it's highly unlikely
you'll achieve both.
the nature of originality
tends to render the two
mutually exclusive.

The Life Force Poems

of course the strongest odds
are that you'll end up
with neither.

i've got to go, though,
with the idea that
the life force is always
the driving force within
the greatest artists
because the life force is,
after all,
what the greatest art
is always all about.

III. THE FORCE

The Life Force Poems

CARMEN

she's always taken what she wanted,
whether or not it belonged to someone else,
and finally it catches up to her.

she's seduced don jose into giving up
his job, his mother, his fiancée,
his comfort, his security, his self-respect
and the respect of others.
she sings a lot about love and freedom,
but he's lost his freedom also-
to jail, to hiding, to her.
he's lost his economic independence.
she's taken everything from him
including the freedom to love and
be loved by anyone else.
how much love do you think
the homeless of any era experience?
she's deprived him of the freedoms
that are guaranteed to those
who live within the law,
freedoms which are not absolute
but which, for most, make life tolerable,
livable, even, perhaps, enjoyable.
the gypsy life is not for everyone
or even for many.

still, biologically,
carmen's singleness of purpose is essential-
the attractive force must summon,
as dylan thomas delineated in
"if i were tickled by the rub of love,"
against all reason,

in the face of all dissuasions:
feuds, vendettas, microbes, impoverishment,
shotgun weddings, loss of "quality of life."
if we ever really started acting rationally
there might never be another child born
(is "planned parenthood" for instance, really
planning _for_ parenthood or _prevention_ of it?)
yeats asks what woman would endure
the pain of giving birth, could she but see
the scarecrow into which the child would age.
who's ever accepted parenthood
out of a considered commitment to
the future of the human race?
neither narcissist nor altruist nor nihilist
chooses procreation.
no, it's sex we are impelled by,
pleasure, ecstasy, release,
within which masquerades
the irrational, _counter_-rational, genetic force-
"the force that through the green fuse
drives the flower," the force that
equally drives _our_ "green age."

later we learn to love
the consequences of our lust.
likewise it's essential men compete
for the most sexually desirable women
and women for the most biologically desirable men.
aggression is a necessary part of the equation,
maybe even violence or, at least,
the threat of it,
the readiness for it.

these are hard words,
but the truth is seldom saccharine,
so we poeticize it.

The Life Force Poems

the forces seldom rest in equilibrium:
the pendulum swings past the center,
touches the extremes before retreating.
we are always striving
to restore a balance.

and yet the tragedy
of carmen and of don jose:
children do not seem to have been
in the cards. perhaps he was
too weak-unworthy of her-perhaps the
matador would have been the ideal
impregnator of carmen-but desire
has destroyed desire. perhaps the
passionate must die, unfit for parenthood,
unless, at last, their passion dies.
should carmen have settled down
with don jose? could she have?

what sort of a mother
would carmen have made?

with the maternal change in hormones
would she not have been
a different carmen?
i've seen a lot of men and women
settle down, from wildness into quiet strength,
and some who couldn't.

i guess it could be said
she gets what she asked for,
what she deserves,
what she must have known
would someday be her portion,
ironically, of course, it comes
just as she seems herself to have,

Gerald Locklin

for the first time in her life,
fallen truly, deeply, madly in love,
perhaps even permanently,
certainly vulnerably.
does don jose <u>save</u> escamillo from carmen
or carmen from escamillo,
or does he come obscenely
in his pettiness, unworthiness, weakness,
between two strengths?

does he save passion from marriage?
keep it separate, as denis de rougemont
says always is the case?

at the end of <u>the sun also rises</u>
has lady brett actually, as she says,
left that later bullfighter, pedro romero,
for his own sake,
or has <u>he</u> dumped <u>her</u>?
after all, whose star is ascending,
and who is the fading rose,
the aging circe,
soon to lose her own power?

would escamillo not have
loved and left carmen?

carmen, the exciter to procreation,
is also the destroyer of the family, of
the institution of the family?

was the man not meant for the home?
was the man meant to roam?
some at least,
not don jose, perhaps, but escamillo?
or is the answer in the sublimation

The Life Force Poems

of one strength into another,
that of the father<u>er</u>
into the father?

what, then, do we make of this?
a caution against extremes,
oversimplification?
the necessity of both passion and society?
freedom and the family?
children in and out of wedlock?
wine and holy water?
the impulsive and the planned?
the sacred and the profane?

freud knew of it,
the id and superego,
civilization and its discontents.
so did darwin:
somehow, outside the laws of "civilized society,"
the gypsies have survived.

where in all of this resides
the military with its disciplines?
its sexual deuteronomy co-existing with
unbridled satisfactions?

at the premiere of <u>carmen</u>,
as at that of
<u>the playboy of the western world</u>,
the audience rioted.

Gerald Locklin

MC COY TYNER TRIO

1. sans souci

at the jazz bakery
they don't even bother
to collect the tickets
at the door,
just as i don't
take roll in my classes.
i'm sure they figure
no real jazz fan
would begrudge such a low-frills
high-class club the support
necessary for survival. and
if a starving student or
old-timer slips in, well,
then, fine. in my case
i refuse to waste my
energies playing policeman.
if my students aren't
motivated to learn, then
who's the loser? surely,
not i. i've already read
the poems and novels, studied
their place in literary history. the
students can choose to acquire
what i already have, or they
can choose to rest in ignorance.
a lot of the things our
parents told us as kids-
that we hated to hear
repeated and later learned to
ridicule-prove to be ironically

The Life Force Poems

true, such as "you're only
hurting yourself." so, it's really
no skin off my ass if a
student chooses to "get away"
with anything-it will catch up
with him in life. but, fortunately,
the majority of my students
are and always have been
hungry to feast at
the banquet of knowledge and
aesthetic pleasure.

2. three musicians

the young bass player,
avery sharpe,
can make the deep strings
sing, though he comports
himself with modesty of rhythm,
as befits his instrument.

the drummer, aaron scott, is
unleashed on an endless solo
far beyond the seeming limits
of athleticism into the realm
where breath and thought suspend
themselves and the spirit is
made sinew.

there's no substitute for experience,
though, maturity, from having backed
miles, coltrane, cannonball.
when the piano adds walls
of arpeggios, tidal waves of
reconciled polarities, the left

hand holding to archetypal as
the right explores the narrative
of history and the present, then
the synchronic and the diachronic
disappear in a massively symphonic
filling-up of the room and of
the consciousness dwelling in it,
as time melts into the eternal.

3. ruth price

still trim and cute
in veiled dress and high heels-
shapely legs and little butt-
how old could she be?
why did she stop performing?
how can she not sing along-
of course she must-she must
be always singing-even i am
always singing, and i seldom
even know the words.
yeats had it, "the aged man
is but a paltry thing
unless soul clap its hands
and sing . . ."

jazz can kill you-it can
also keep you young-keep
you from ever dying?

The Life Force Poems

A COMER: CARLOS MCKINNEY WITH ELVIS JONES

you know, i actually took piano lessons
from second grade until
the end of high school.
i never got any good at it-
i could read sheet music fine,
but had little muscle control,
couldn't pick out "happy birthday" by ear,
never understood harmony,
and was terrified of having to perform
anything from memory
or of being asked to transpose a work
into an unwritten key.
but i did get a lot of pleasure
out of sitting long hours at the piano
evoking for myself with rhapsodic gusto
those pieces i had been taught to play
from the sheet music,
especially after one of the nuns
encouraged me to pick out popular songs
at the music store
with which to alternate the prescribed classics.

i also for a time
got it into my head
to study the drums-
and i might have been
a little better at them-
i do have a tolerable grasp of rhythm.
but my mother's answer was:
"you don't even practice the piano-
why add a second instrument?"
it was the only time i can remember

ever having been deprived of
an educational opportunity.
anyway, before going off to college,
i not only quit taking piano lessons
but actually quit playing the piano altogether-
i made a concrete, considered decision
to forego wasting countless hours
doing something at which i would always be mediocre
when i could be trying to excel at writing
and could also be enjoying

the work of musicians
much more talented than myself.

then last night i heard a young pianist and composer,
carlos mckinney,
perform at the jazz bakery
with the elvin jones jazz machine.
it was an incredible display
of keyboard mastery,
of intelligence, strength, spontaneity, and soul,
especially the pounding, slapping, rubato chords
of the right hand.
it was like being witness to
the youthful mccoy tyner
coming into his own
and into the pantheon
with the john coltrane of <u>a love supreme</u>.

you could tell elvin jones
(who was very much <u>there</u> in those days)
felt the same way as the audience-
he was at his best when accompanying
the piano improvisations
and was grinning and muttering
like any proud papa.

The Life Force Poems

it was a memorable evening,
before a packed house,
replete with standing ovations,
for the youth as well as the mentor,

and it was a redeeming night as well:

because i drove home vindicated
that i had made the right decision
in giving up the piano
and that my mother
had done me a great favor
in denying me the drums.

DUET: JUNE CHRISTY AND STAN KENTON

look at her on the cover of this album
that i first interminably played
as a high-school sophomore in 1955:
schoolgirl-pretty and schoolgirl-innocent,
bobbed hair, bare shoulders,
and sufficient bosom,
knees crossed beneath a chaste white skirt,
hands clasped upon her legs.
her lips are parted in
an almost-smile into the spotlight.

no wonder i was taken with her:
she was the high-school sweetheart
i was searching for
and soon would find.

how many torch songs i encountered
for the first time on that

33 1/3 rpm vinyl platter:
"ev'ry time we say goodbye,"
"lonely woman,"
"angel eyes,"
"baby, baby all the time,"
"how long has this been going on,"
and of course one i already knew
from <u>the king and i</u>: "we kiss in a shadow."

and the liner notes detail
the sheer determination with which
the teenager from decatur, illinois,
armed with her demo,
outwitted the bandleader
in the chicago waiting room
of general artists corporation.
pure naive pursual of a dream,
but kierkegaard said
"purity of heart is
oneness of intention."

The voice betrays a worldly understanding though-
a duskiness of instinct or experience.
other favorites of mine-
polly bergen, julie london, judy garland-
had this earthy quality combined
with perfect pitch as well-
and also the idiosyncratic repertoire-
but christy was the girl next door.
(though not next door to me).

will friedwald speaks of
the nakedness of the project,
neither of the artists known as virtuoso,
both self-critical to an extreme,
and kenton certainly not given to

The Life Force Poems

the self-effacement of accompanist.

(the memorable titles of his compositions
come to mind: for instance,
"concerto to end all concertos."
chuck niles says, "stan always
did think big.")

here, though, he sits to one side,
eyes downcast, the most incidental,
almost accidental of svengalis.
perhaps he was in love with her.
or hot for her at least-
for what a tableau of 1950's sexuality:
the girl next door
singing naked in the garden.
talk about your sex objects!
talk about the gaze of the voyeur!
talk about old fashioned, sinful, oh-so-healthy lust!

strangely, those good old days
didn't seem so great at the time.

but now i have this re-release
because our later years are partly
the rekindling of our early loves.

my son comes from his room
to say "who's that?
she's good.
great voice."

"i know," i say, "and yet
apparently she always
lacked self-confidence."

"but he believed in her?"

"it sounds like it;
it damn well sounds like it,
and, ultimately, in himself."

THE COOLEST CATS ON THE CHOPPING BLOCK

i got to thinking about
what might be the coolest
record ever. i think
i was listening to "the girl
from ipanema" at the time,
the sax-voice of stan getz
and the human voice of astrud gilberto
almost interchangeable, weaving around
each other like slightly woozy
cobras, or soon-to-be-lovers
sizing each other up.

obvious candidates would have to be
almost any cut on brubeck's <u>time out</u>,
brimming with sustained precision,
brilliant rhythmic variations,
every tendency towards ostentation
held in check to where restraint
itself became the tour-de-force.

ahmad jamal on "poinciana,"
an extended meditation,
every note and chord in place,
dynamics kept in perfect range:

"my funny valentine,"

The Life Force Poems

with chet and gerry mulligan?
a tad too sentimental
for our category?
"solea" from <u>sketches of spain</u>?
again, a classic, but perhaps
too close to brimming over with
miles' fuming passion and
that of the spanish people?

something by the m.j.q.?
almost anything?
their updated versions of bach?

or how about the vocalists?
billie, nat, or frank,
who, in the face of what
life flung at them, kept their musical
cools, as they stepped,
at their own dignified paces,
never, in their art,
out of control,
toward death.

even the flamboyant kenton,
the leonine, symphonic stan,
had his quiet moments
of duet with julie christie.

cool is not the only
kind of jazz, but it provides
a measured classicism
lyric yet formal,
bounded yet intense,
that you can listen to
time and again,
without the saccharine

embarrassment of excess,
the cloying dissonance
of pity. it is art's
refusal to be overwhelmed.
it says emotion and intelligence
need not exclude each other.

HOLY THURSDAY

i go to hear
the young brazilian pianist, helio alves,
at the jazz bakery, with a trio
completed by wilson matta on bass
and duduka da fonseca on drums,
both of the trio da paz,
and it's an ill-scheduled date,
both holy thursday and passover,
which means i'm one of only
eight or nine in the audience,
but this doesn't inhibit the
joyous working-out of the virtuosi,
especially the two-fisted,
two-footed layers of chords,
waves of glissandi,
stacks of arpeggios,
applied by the talented, schooled,
inventive, and inspired
young maestro of the pianoforte-

and that, of course, is what
live jazz has always been,
the friendly competition that drives
each member of a group

The Life Force Poems

beyond what one might have
thought one's limits were,
making something for the immortal moment,
a legendary evening,
a performance not to be forgotten,
even if recorded only in the
circuits and the fibers of the
players and their audience who
come to work as one in the
athleticism and aestheticism of the
timeless, time-stamped instant
(which is nonetheless about time
and the extent to which man
may aspire to master that which
ultimately masters him)-
the dance of shiva, inner dance
of all, dance of the dancer
live within our sluggish daily lives,
dance of the stopped time when
we become the most alive
that we will ever be . . .

and so, after the set,
before going out to my car,
in the rain, i purchase at
the counter two c.d.'s:
<u>trios</u> and <u>partido out</u>,

but when the next day and
the next week i start to listen to
them-bossas, be-bops, ballads,
standards-they are cool and
excellent-i'll listen to them
often-but they aren't the
evening that i bought them to
remind me of-they aren't

the passion, conflagration,
uninhibited infinitude of the
live jazz explosion, life-beyond-
life, eternity-within-a-
second, something william
blake invented a century before
eubie blake, before ruben gonzales,
arsenio rodriguez . . .

and i realize it's something
i have missed on other albums also,
flawless as they were for their purposes,
the studied perfection of the
studio . . .

listening to recordings of
danilo perez, mc coy tyner,
ahmad jamal, after hearing
them in person, not a
matter of the inferior
but of difference, a different
kind of pleasure, contemplation,
that one learns to settle for,
to take for what it is,
which is a lot-which can
be the sublime:

who, for instance, would want
the gil evans/ miles davis <u>sketches</u>
or <u>porgy</u> to be anything other
than what they are-classics
for all time and of all time
(that word <u>time</u> again!) . . .

and yet there <u>is</u> a different
kind of classic too: the

The Life Force Poems

live recording of <u>ellington</u> at
<u>newport</u>, paul gonsalves
crazy on <u>diminuendo and crescendo
in blue</u>, going far beyond
himself, crossing a line into
places he'd never been before,
might never go again,
or maybe, in his own soul,
never quite returned from . . .

different modes of beauty.
varying intensities of meditation,
different ways to love oneself,
becoming more oneself than one
has ever been . . .

but where has one found
the live still living recently:

largely in the cuban:
chucho valdez: <u>bele</u>, <u>bele</u>,
the habana of roy hargrove's <u>cristol</u>,
the return, in memory, of
judy garland to carnegie,
chet and gerry to that selfsame <u>hall</u> . . .

but really, i suppose, to find
the live, we have to go to it,
we have to live it,
give ourselves to it,
our lives to it . . .

our children know this,
know it now,
and they, like us, will
have to go forth all their

lives to keep re-learning it-

the dance, the dance,
the dance upon the grecian urn,
the dance of the syllables,
the dance of life and death,
the lonely frozen blazing dance
that is eternity.

THE NICHOLAS PAYTON QUINTET AT THE JAZZ BAKERY

he wears a suit and tie,

i almost never do.
maybe ten times in four decades.
no disrespect intended.
i grew up dressing up
for catholic school,
and now i've gotten used to comfort.

but he looks comfortable
in suit and tie, and it certainly
is not interfering with his credibility.

it may have been at one time
a necessity for black musicians
to show respect,
to gain respect.
i think we've bid farewell now
to the cotton club.

i don't listen to music
when i'm doing something else
requiring concentration.

The Life Force Poems

i listen to music,
at home alone,
or in my car,
or here.

is there any woman that i wish
were here with me?
one comes to mind.
another.
maybe a third.
but none are necessary.
if i were ever to go anywhere, though,
with the one,
or the other,
or the third,
this might be
as good a place as any.

TIM WARFIELD

this saxophonist is quite young,
but no sax player is ever really young.

sax players have died young,
but sax players do not die.

we bald,
and we become emboldened.

coltrane sought (and found)
a love supreme.

now this young man,
like coltrane,

is not simply doing
what he knows
that he can do,
not just going beyond
what we might
imagine he could do,
but setting forth
to go beyond
what even he
thinks he could
ever possibly
uncover.

the re-invention of the self
and of the song,
as we become
who we were meant to be,
and come full circle to
the music of concentric spheres.

IF I WERE A PAINTER

i would paint a picture,
representational or abstract,
of <u>black men wearing hats</u>.

many are not losing hair.
the gentleman a row in front of me
removes his, unrequested, so as not
to block the view of a
middle-aged white woman.

one wears his with a jaunt.
some seem inseparable.

The Life Force Poems

some make a statement:
dare to touch it,
ridicule it,
even stare at it.
i knew one once
concealed a razor blade.

i haven't worn, or owned,
a real hat since a fedora
with a feather in the band
that i wore to
the easter parade,
fifth avenue,
across from st. patrick's,
at the age of-
what-
eight? nine?
i guess that i'd seen
fred astaire with judy garland.

now even yankees' caps
fly off,
unseat my glasses,
are alien.

but it is as it should be
that a few black men
wear pork pies, derbies, even bowlers,

escorting lady-friends to jazz.

Gerald Locklin

SLIDE

the early days of be-bop
were before my time,
but listening to the great trombonist,
a slightly second-generation protege
of bird and diz and bud,
now master to a new generation
of young turks, you realize that
joy was the essence of it,
playing fast and furious and
changing streetcars on the run,
the unadulterated fun of it,
the jet-age waiting on the runway,
the new-found freedoms grafted onto
roots of field songs, blues, and
spirituals, and the urban voyage of
discovery up and down the black and white
keys of the mississippi-
n'orlins, st. louis, chicago--
spreading wings then east to harlem,
west to central avenue,
rites of passage back across both oceans,
sheer excitement of the opening up of it,
the glimpses of untold possibilities,
the scalding chill of what infinity might be.

miles and monk and chet and coltrane--
they'd usher in a different consciousness,
postwar parisian existentialism,
journey inward,
exploration of the self,
the symphony of mind,

The Life Force Poems

search for the elusive blue note,
the <u>ineffable</u> of mallarmé and baudelaire,
the chordal confrontation with resurgence
of a life lived only once,
the intimation that this freedom

was an all, an everything, an
inescapable condition, something
from which there was no retreat
but only the totality of an
evolving orchestration,
the supreme love,
darkness at each end of it.

in the days before the war, though,
in the days when an america refused
to be depressed by a depression,
there was confirmation of
the ornithology
of the unorthodox,
an escalation, exhalation,
expectation, exaltation.

doesn't matter how young bird died--
read walter pater,
read the life of christ.

jazz is about origins and endings,
which, as that aficionado of cool cats,
tom eliot, discovered in gardened, country
churchyards, hewn upon the mossy stones,
are one.

Gerald Locklin

CHAIM SOUTINE: HILL AT CÉRET

the earth's a charnal house.
we dwell with maggot-microbes.
the molecules of rotting never rest.
even rocks rot.

i am myself a graveyard,
mind as well as body,
and my soul a beetle
on the heap of shit
i manufacture.

with age our greatest aspiration
is efficient defecation.

on a successful day
we do not shit our pants.

and yet blood is lava,
sweat rises,
and the struck brain
is a thunderstorm,
an atom split or spliced.

TWO ALONE

the woman who sits next to me
is not a beauty, but she's not
bad-looking either, casually dressed and
younger than myself. somehow

The Life Force Poems

we got into discussing baseball,
whether the cubs, down two games to
none in a post-season series, can
come back at home. how she hates
my yankees. good news about
darryl strawberry's cancer surgery;
bad news in dan quisenberry's
early death. i wonder if she's
as alone as she seems to be,
if she comes to these things by
herself as i do, or if she's with
one of the musicians, or has hopes
of being. i wouldn't mind meeting
her here sometime when i'd have a
little more time afterward, maybe
build a bit of a relationship around
a mutual appreciation of the music.

at intermission i lose track of her
until i look up from a newspaper
to find her sipping soup
at the table next to mine.

for the second set she doesn't
return to our row, sits down
front instead, but she does
sit one seat in, leaves
the aisle seat empty.
a few minutes later though,
i see her go to the backstage
door, open it tentatively,
say a word or two to
someone inside.

yeah, i was right not

to get any notions into my
head, not to move up into
that seat next to hers
and risk making a fool of
myself.

no fool, they say,
like an old fool.

of course, one form of
foolishness is fear of
looking foolish.

in my time i have been
both kinds of fool.

PICASSO 2000

> "he went for the strongest level of feeling, staking everything,
> on sensation and desire." --robert hughes

desire is its many meanings;
thus, desire is a mandolin with
girl. desire is the green
savannah that has only known
the sun. beside a pineapple, a
bottle turns green with desire.
two blocks of women, one of
them a man with breasts, evince
the terror and invasion of
desire, while, in avignon, the
dames are both desired and

The Life Force Poems

desirous and the vast inversion
of blue ice. desire has the
power to turn a man into a
minotaur, a woman into sylvan
satire. desire doth reject the
ruler and the ruled, the eden-
garden and the english. desire
is perpetually quenched/rekindled.

a woman's face is many faces,
and her movement is not linear.

his friends were poets and musicians.

he taught the painters to un-see,
the sculptors to construct.

he was a hunter/gatherer,
impatient of moss.

the minotaur must lead the maiden
into and out of the house of mirrors.
the maiden must lead the minotaur
out of and into the house of mirrors.
a mirror is a surface of surprising depth.

he sapped his women and survived them.
no woman-artist was his equal.
he made his women
lethal, ugly, and immortal.
at 53 he cast in bronze
a she-goat out of palm leaf,
pots, a wicker basket, scraps
and plaster.
at 91, he died,

a child at play.

MICHAEL SERRA: <u>TORQUED ELLIPSE</u>

the universe is not square.
light is not a line,
your neck twists and turns,
you change and stay the same,

oxygen acts upon us.
we go around, but
not exactly in circles.
we open cans.

we see up but not out.
we are a maze,
made up of mazes,
and we're <u>in</u> a maze,
made up of mazes,
which is in a maze.

<u>et cetera</u>.

we like things bigger than ourselves.
we like to get to the bottom of things
(e.g. the grand canyon)
and look up.
we like to get to the top of things
(e.g. everest)
and look down.

we like the old,
but we also like the new.

The Life Force Poems

we like our artists to
remember the old
while making it new.
(e.g. the cantos, the waste land,
ulysses, the waves.)
we like to see time given space.
we like to walk
inside ourselves.

we uncurl into the world
and curl up into sleep,
and sleep itself is a curl.

candy curls.

craters.
crucibles.
perhaps giant pastas.
cathedrals.
catafalques.

our lives are torqued by these.

MAN RAY: BLANC ET NOIR

the critic says this photo
isn't pornographic because
pornography is always deadly
serious? is he kidding? has
he ever cracked de sade or
glommed a single porno flick?
humor has always been a scam
for legitimizing the erotic, letting

us feel superior to the things
that turn us on, pretending that
they don't. so i'm not supposed
to find this woman with the narrow
gypsy chin and sloppy silken hose
exciting, her bare nipples and
thighs contrasted to the bands and
garters, shoes and lips of black. i'm
supposed to recognize the work as
a reduction to absurdity of "the
objectification of women," and be
rendered inert by its "hilarity,"
"self-parody," its postmodernism ahead
of its time.

doesn't this guy know that the
objectification of women _is_ exciting,
is _supposed_ to be? it's not
the _whole_ relationship to women,
but it _is_ a _part_ of it.

no, i think he doesn't.

call it a cheap shot,
but i don't think he has to
worry a whole hellova lot
about objectifying women,
except perhaps his mother.

man ray knew better,
knew it from brooklyn to berlin.

The Life Force Poems

JOSEPH NOEL PASTOR: THE QUARREL OF OBERON AND TITANIA

first of all you have to understand
that, even were i so inclined, i
don't possess enough left brain
to paint my toenails accurately.
thus, taste be damned: how can
i help but be impressed by paintings
with a couple hundred fairies gamboling
in rings and pairs and trios. moreover,
take a gander at the lovely titties,
hairless pussies, of these gossamer-
winged delicacies. the critic says
they can't have "real sex," and i guess
that he means intercourse by that,
but whatever kind of sex they're
having sure does hold the eye.
look at the couple in the foreground,
rolling in each other's arms, teasing
nipples and the corner of the mouth.
into what private, fleshy bower is
that more mature and gemmed one
leading the teenager, fingers in the
golden locks behind her neck? clearly
what we have here is the moment of
anticipation just before the deeds
themselves, the tension wound up to
its tightest twist, before the springing.
and any gal who isn't doing is engrossed
in watching (or is contemplating
joining in). the critic says it's
"fun"-well, he's got that right!
i wouldn't mind a little such

abandonment myself-this is one eden
where i doubt i'd be distracted
by the plants. i sure hope that the
arbitrator takes his time in getting
this dispute resolved. in the meantime
i'll just stand over here, out of
the way, up against this whatchamacallit
tree. don't pay me any nevermind.
if you need me in your consciousness
just call-otherwise, I'll just make
your world part of mine.

JACKSON POLLOCK: <u>BLUE POLES</u>, NUMBER 11, 1952

winter, i think, at first;
a bright winter day,
dormant wheat of winter,
crust of hibernation,
the single, final, cracking chord
of a frozen upstate symphony.

crystals, icicles, patches of snow.
light without heat.
the red of holiday cheer,
of barnyard sacrifice.
pale blue of fingertips, thermometers.
strips of frost.
the yellow of dead frogs.

and the poles so blue as
almost to be black,
tribal sceptres, patriarchal staffs,
lodgepole pines,

The Life Force Poems

fence-poles of frozen corn fields,
needing the repair of april,
draped with wire, electrically barked.

drums along the mohawk,
lances in a lonely child's imagination.

a december of the mind,
there and in memory,

or,

the magnetic moment,
gyromagnetic ratio,
angular momentum:

stasis of the electromagnetic spectrum.

the artist, unthinking; serves science,
becomes its lightning rod,
wordless poet of the mathematical,
speaker of the felt/unseen,
mind galvanized.
the answer is always
all of the above.

THE WAR GOES ON

i read in tony hillerman's
navajo reservation novel,
<u>the first eagle</u>, confirmation of
news stories concerning how the bacteria
of plague, streptococcus, and

tuberculosis are becoming resistant to
our traditional antibiotics, and our
immune systems cannot fight off the
hantavirus,

     but that same night i
read in wilson's <u>consilience</u>
that public demand, as expressed through
our elected representatives, has channeled
funding in scientific research toward work on
genetic engineering and other facets of
molecular biology that could result in
the prevention and curing of diseases.

A MESSAGE GONE AWRY

i overhear a man about my age say
"if not now, when?"
i wonder if he heard that first,
as i did, from peter marin,
with whom i taught at l.a. state
in 1964-65. he was right, of course,
some people postpone living in an endless
preparation for a life that leaks its fuel before it
fires from its launching pad.
prufrock, for instance, and john marcher.
newman's <u>idea of a university</u>:
make it as close to life as possible;
you only learn to live by living.

still, all ideas go too far: the wise youth
does defer a few things while arming
himself for the fray, takes his

The Life Force Poems

lessons gradually, doesn't take foolhardy
risks, doesn't strike out to do battle
with or tame the sharks until he's
learned to swim. we inner-directed children of the
cautious 50's needed to be urged
to act, but all too many of the
very young have perished in the decades since,
impetuously, and from acting far beyond
their age, or any age.

# The Life Force Poems

IV. ART AND LIFE

BLOOMSBURY

you didn't have to be that talented
to be an artist
or that beautiful
to have a sex life
or that sexual to have
the romance, drama, lyricism
of entanglements.
you could have a family
or simply be a part of one.
if you were a stay-at-home
you could make your home
your work of art.
you could cultivate
both privacy and hospitality.
bisexuality made perfect sense.
so did pacifism.
so did the omega workshops,
picking up where william morris
left off.
nature could be
your own backyard.
books were as real
as journalism.
book reviews mattered.
children were contextualized.
the painters weren't as great
as the post-impressionists they
popularized and interpolated
but they were fortunate enough
to have <u>writers </u>in the group
who <u>were</u> world class.

Gerald Locklin

and they were smart enough
to do their portraits
even if, sometimes, they forgot
to paint the faces in.

vanessa bell did not forget
to pillory the visage of
lady ottoline morrell, not to mention
that of her husband's mistress.
free love was supposed to reign,
deceit and jealousy be banned,
but are they ever?
we try to blame our fallen nature
on society
and figment our emotional autopsies,
but we cannot eradicate our
epigenetic predisposition.
programmed to compete, survive,
we can only dissemble our emotions,
sometimes sublimate them,
substitute passive aggression
for outright hostility.
thus do our camelots become dystopias.
only dora carrington, outsider,
had the power and the passion.
the others had their pride of
place, of education, breeding,
influence, eloquence, etiquette.
but the fire was lacking in them.
maybe eliot, a hogarth author,
sensed in them, as in himself,
the hollowness, the lack.
how beautiful the opening of
<u>the wasteland</u>, though, the
modern music of that page

The Life Force Poems

laid open in the glass case
just across the gallery from
the prose sinuosities of the
first page of the preface to
the <u>eminent victorians</u> of lytton
strachey-and how <u>he</u> looked
exactly as he should-and
<u>would</u> as portrayed by jonathan pryce
(these art directors do their field work)
and how the men all crossed
their legs like women.
somehow they managed to procreate, though,
and still do. a dynasty
and cottage industry
abetted by those of aesthetic affinity,
of a spiritual, perhaps sexual kinship,
andrew lloyd webber springs to mind,
the ageless aspects of love.

and angelica bell is alive still,
in her 90's and i'm only
two degrees of separation from her
<u>via</u> julian bell and brian hinton
and i've been to st. ives where
as children they played, maybe posed,
upon the sand of studland beach. and
i have stayed on gower street near
all the squares of gordon, bedford, russell, tavistock.
monk's house, charleston farm,
knole, sissinghurst. read freud
in the laconic, un-lacanic sentences of
strachey, james.
(he and his wife, alix, and
adrien stephen all became lay analysts.)
i will continue to be drawn to them,

dragged to them, sometimes, by
my wife, who knows their
lives and everything unliterary they
produced much better than i do,
who would perhaps have been a
good deal happier with them,
or maybe only thinks so.

and at the end
i will have learned
as the ol'possum did
what any child knows
screaming into the surroundings
he will try to make a world
of, habitat for what
he'll hang his name on:
it's not easy to be human,
and the humaner you try to be
the harder it will get.

SAN RAMON PASTORAL

what an uncharacteristically romantic
and literarily pretentious thing
for me to have done:
i've turned off a baseball game,
put down an updike,
and descended to the side of
the hotel pool with a spiral notebook
and a marriott pen
to jot these lines.
i don't think i've <u>ever</u>
written poolside before,

The Life Force Poems

hotel or otherwise.

but i wasn't looking for inspiration.
i already have that.
i returned a while ago
from an hour's walk around what used to be
bishop's ranch, here in san ramon,
in the san ramon valley.

there used to be steinbeck hills,
a cup of gold,
a garden of the sun,
now both green and bronze.
near the end of
this unpredictable <u>la niña</u> june.
i could see el diablo on my walk,
but it didn't seem anything like
a devil mountain to me;
not threatening, foreboding, crackling
like one you'd expect in the carpathians
or rip van winkle's catskills,
not even as steep a walk as
arthur's mount, outside glastonbury,
although higher no doubt.
no, it seemed gentle, rounded, feminine,
as refreshing as everything else about
my constitutional:
the brisk warm wind through crow canyon
into norris canyon;
the only slightly rolling path
around the corporate headquarters of
pac bell, toyota, chevron;

the weekend quiet of
these industrial estates;

Gerald Locklin

the duck and geese undisturbed by the passage
of an occasional jogger or stroller.
credit where credit is due:
those big businesses have done their best
to reinstate, if not preserve,
the beauty of this place.
the grounds remind me of paris:
patterned gravel walks,
shrouded by arcades of aspens,
gas pumps tucked discreetly behind
an earth-toned wall;
a long reflecting pond
so rippled by the wind
and crested by the waterfowl
that you would swear it wasn't artificial;
landscaped grassy knolls,
untrampled as a virgin golf course,
an evening that a wordsworth, emerson, thoreau,
might, just might,
(given the century,
given the turning of the century)
just might have been as able as i have
to take peace and contemplation from
(and badly needed endorphins).

the thoughts were not all tranquil:
love, as for a child, always
implies anxiety;

intensity of life is wedded to,
as wallace stevens knew,
mortality;
one friend surprises you with benefaction
as another slips the poniard 'twixt
the drying vertebrae.

The Life Force Poems

and marriage, well ...
well, i return to that,
for better or for worse
for ever or a day,
tomorrow.

i'd hoped there might be lovely women
in or by the pool
but there are only kids in fins and goggles.
i guess god saved me from distraction.
the sun has gone behind the pine trees
that conceal the massive
and convenient, eminently human
discount store.

it's time to go inside.
i may step in the exercise room,
small, adjoining,
for a set or two
of curls and presses,
kid myself that i am still
a kid.

and do i wish i were?
oh, hell, you know,
my life's been far from perfect
and i've hurt a lot of people that i loved
but i'm not sure i could design a better one,
not even if i could begin again
with everything i've learned.

frankly i don't even know
what advice to give
my son who's going off to
college in the fall.

i'll tell my self that there are things
i really should pass on to him,
wisdom squeezed from needless suffering-

i'll even think i've got it phrased just right-

and then the time is just not right-

or i'm afraid i'll do more harm than good-

like prufrock i recall polonius

and my son is probably relieved
i leave his life to him.

there is a chill upon the night now,
where there was a warmth.
updike, diet pepsi, and the baseball scores await.
pleasures not to be disparaged.

i see a lady getting in the sauna,
svelte, a one-piece bathing suit,
forty, a mother, fighting to retain
the dignity of bodily appearance that
we so briefly are allowed.

i'll pass her as i leave,
permit my astigmatic eyes to linger:

another under-rated pleasure,
gift of shiva,
given with the right hand,
taken with the left.

The Life Force Poems

MARC CHAGALL: A SEQUENCE OF POEMS
the canopy (huppa), 1912

the wind is in the willows,
and the willow is a woman.

when there's smoke there's fire,
and the smoke is sky-blue-pink beneath
the canopy of stars.

let *our* canopy be daylight colors,
green and citrus; let the adolescent
boys uphold the posts.

elders, take pride in your beards,
the prime of life to which we will
aspire.

love knocks the lovers off their feet.
let there be witnesses; let them
share our joy.

even oscar wilde loved weddings.

a pinch of snuff 1912

all stars are six-pointed.
no stars have six points.

pinch of snuff gives respite from the torah.
and inspiration?

the jews and arabs, greeks and
asians knew the highest labor was
of intellect. the irish knew it
also. but the romans?

yes, a beard is green. a beard
is emerald as a window-sash.
the wind, therefore, attires itself in black.

our brows grow furrowed as our fields.
our cry of intellectual joy is yellow.

we have two lines of succession:
one hoards gold and one is golden.
why value anything that can be taken
from you? give all to the children;
give all to the poor; give all you have
to life. the conqueror conquers dust.

cemetery gates, 1917

the revolutions of the warlords
will not raise us from the dead.

only the animals can intercede for us.
we must learn from our ghosts.
we must grow like joseph,
vinelike from the earth.
let us shatter all shapes, and
reconfigurate them as they fall and fly.
the sky takes its color from the eye.

learn from the fly to walk up walls.
see through the ceilings to the
open tabernacle of the night.

The Life Force Poems

give gifts on purim, savor sweets.

a man may write or paint on any
plane or surface, slant or level.

so much depends on the water-bearer.

change colors with the cycle of the
seasons; learn when to hibernate and
when to be reborn.

what black-eyed rodent seeks to row us
to the other life?

some dead are deader than others.

paris is a coney island of the mind;
so is vitebsk.

the cemetery gates are always open;
come and go as you please.

a heart is full; its gates are open.

the green violinist

sometimes he was red.
he was not always on the roof.
but he was always all they had of
melody, of dance, of where they
came from, places that their ancestors
had seen, sacred and profane.

he raised the dead;
he rid the death from all of them.

Gerald Locklin

his coat was constructed by braque;
he was paris in vitebsk.

feast day (rabbi with lemon)

his beard is as black as the air
inside the temple. it is where
he always goes; it is where
they have gone for centuries. it
is where they go together.

and yet his pungent gift of the taste
of life seems poignantly unwelcome.

he seems a gentle loving man, who
wants to worship god, as of old.

is anyone at home? what year was
samuel beckett born?

his other self, on the top of his
head, turns away.

man walking, 1918

a man walks back upon himself,
with checkered pants by mondrian.

a giant step towards freedom?

or a goosestep towards postmodernism.

The Life Force Poems

bella with white collar

we need a woman to look over us
and our children
in the forest of our days,
the jungle of our nights.

it is not exactly what graves meant
by his white goddess; it is closer to
the mother of us all,
the guardian angel.

it is what the modern woman
does not want to be,
or thinks she shouldn't be,
but what will be left
for her to rule?

the gray house

i always liked vitebsk best
when i was not there.

AT THE OPERA

the don juan story
is permanently engaging
because a part of every man
would love to be as successful

in love as the libertine, while
another part fears being the victim
of those predations, not the seduced,
but the cuckolded, the fool,
the lesser man—the pimp or eunuch.

correspondingly, a part of every woman
wants to conquer don juan's promiscuity,
to claim him for her own (trying not
to notice that, domesticated, don
juan is no longer don juan), or, at
the very least, not to be left off his
list (how undesirable must a woman be to
not even be coveted by a satyr?), while
another part will always rage against and
wish to damn or castrate this monster to
whom she is no more than a vagina, a
number, a competing ego to be flattered,
deceived, betrayed, humiliated, abandoned.

the feminists must hate don juan
who denies their sexual agency,
laughs at it, in fact,
derides it, turns it to his
own advantage.

the id and the super-ego,
procreation and civilization,
the penis and the pussy,
always in competition,
always bobbing on the teeter-totter
of hegemony that must, for a society to
survive, find resolution in a harmony.

The Life Force Poems

DAY TRIPS

my wife and i go to museums
by ourselves now, the children
both in college. we drive up
to the getty, hancock park,
the shadow of the coliseum, to
appreciate pop artists and
impressionists, dinosaurs and
eighteenth century actresses,
butterflies that are not free,
but quite affordable, accessible.
we do our best on these days
to be on our best behavior,
tread around each other's toes,
avoid the conflicts etched too
deep for reconciliation, joke
but gently, practice patience, be
agreeable, listen to the
other's tales of workplace stress,
listen to the music that we
think the other'd like to, eat
at places that we think the
other'd like to, join in
condemnation of the other drivers
on the freeway, idiots and morons.
before we leave we do the morning
things we really need or want to do.
if i can get a little swim in,
i'll be more relaxed all day, or
if we walk the dog, we'll both feel
better and won't have that task awaiting
us when we get home. we may go

Gerald Locklin

to el chollo, on western north of pico,
for the sweet green-corn tamales that
are only served from may until
october, feel that we are in an
earlier l.a. we may drive back on
surface roads, through the garment
district, south on central past the
dunbar hotel of the former jazz
scene, soul-food restaurants and
storefront churches, walter mosley's

novelistic turf, and further south
a brief trip to the cul-de-sac that
borders the watts towers, now
fenced off for a preservationist effort,
and watts more of a neighborhood
than white folks realize, a
sleepy, multi-racial village when
radio came there in the 1920's,
once a stop along the old electric
line, the red cars, now the same
along the blue line, rapid transit,
bordered by the major arteries of
century, imperial, wilmington,
and avalon, where a traffic stop
on a hot summer night set
off burn, baby, burn, a third
of a century ago, the first year
i was teaching in l.a., summer
school at l.a. state.

or maybe it's a trip to
the hollywood bowl,
for varèse and a video
show, or to

The Life Force Poems

<u>play on</u>, the ellington and
shakespeare musical at the
historic pasadena playhouse.

maybe someplace to eat cuban
food or indian or salvadoran.
whatever.

these are our good days;
we take pleasure in them
and invest our future in them.
we fill time on freeways
making plans for home repairs,
long overdue, for trips we may
be able to afford next summer.
taking pleasure in how well our
kids are doing, mutually
re-assuring that they will
continue to.
                                  we've
been together thirty years,
and it has been a war,
but not all bad, like
france and england all those
centuries, so close, so far,
so far, so close, so
different. so alike.

if we were ever to go
separate ways it would be
now. i'm sure she knows
this also. it might be better
in the long run, but i'm
sure that we both fear it.
for now the summer's about

over and we'll be too busy
with our jobs to fight much,
neither will be able to afford
the trauma of disruptions, and
we both fear what it might
do to the progress of the kids,
who've been our lives the
last two decades. i hope we'll
have our days like this, though,
days that help recall the
way we started out, the
reasons why we ended up together.
we always liked trips to l.a.
we always made them special days.

The Life Force Poems

V. HAPPINESS

The Life Force Poems

GREEN CORN TAMALES

first in tucson,
now at el cholo in l.a.
on western just south of olympic,
my wife and i make a point
of enjoying them once a summer.

all tamales are not hot,
these are sweet with the syrup
of young corn, steamed within
the husks. even the thin strand
of a green pepper seems sweet.
even the morsel of tender chicken
seems sweet.

sweet as sweethearts
on the evening promenade
above the beach at mazatlan.
sweet as summer evenings.
sweet as the respite, the
renewal, at the end of day.

think sweetly of green corn tamales,
remembering that the water of the desert,
hoarded by the thirsty cactus,
is the sweetest water.

Gerald Locklin

ALFRED STEIGLITZ: THE FLATIRON BUILDING, 1902

it was still a landmark in the 1940s
when my aunts introduced me to new york.
but the trees and park were gone by then,
the benches and paths, the leaves,
the snow upon the branches.
it had become just one more skyscraper
in a forest of them,
different, of course, distinctive,
one might even say distinguished,
but antiquated, and not really very tall.

in this photo, though,
it is still as much a part of nature
as salisbury cathedral across the water meadows,
with even the same coloration
as the wintry twigs,
and of the same degree of thinness, grace.
it could have swayed with the breeze.

as our century commenced,
a few visionaries,
steiglitz, stanford white,
must have imagined that
the works of man
and those of god
could co-exist,
in harmony, and use, and beauty.

The Life Force Poems

THE SPIRITS OF HAVANA

1.

the little kid on congas,
daphnis rodrigues,
couldn't be twelve years old.
at first i think he must be
a midget, and i wonder if,
hidden by drums,
his feet even reach the floor.

the leader and saxophonist,
jane bunnett, quips that he is
out of school for the summer,
but once the music starts, you
realize this boy doesn't need any
school except that of pancho quinto,
his weatherbeaten, expressionless mentor,
next to him on timbales
and later on the sacred batas.
young daphnis has small hands still
but big-league heart and instincts.
he throws his head back
and shuts his eyes,
the better to listen to
his history, his blood, his universe.
the others in the outfit have to smile
at his confidence, absorption,
utter lack of any doubt that he belongs,
deserves to be exactly where he is.
he and his spiritual (actual?)
grandfather are as black as santeria,

as orpheus, as the gorge of oldovai.

2.

did music come first or did language?
poetry or passion? voice or gesture?
eve or lilith? time or the eternal?
man or god or something else?
all dissolve in the aesthetic.

3.

here we have
the old man and the sea,
santiago and the boy,
brought off the page alive
before our eyes.

no wonder hemingway preceded
boundaries of nations and religions.
he was a scripturalist
of the oldest testament.
he listened to origins.

4.

when the time comes to
join hands for the final bow,

the boy will not come forward
until the ancient one is helped to
his feet and led, stiff and stooping,
to the forefront.

The Life Force Poems

5.

we learn nothing from our old,
presume instead to teach them
how to pass their dwindling days
in the mindlessness of games or television,
elevator music for their requiems,
until this life is indistinguishable
from the ozone/nozone of
no life at all.

6.

our young men run in packs.

THE FORMIDABLE GEORGE COLEMAN

he's a strong man,
a trifle slow of gait now,
but big of chest and biceps,
and, for his age, relatively
narrow of waist.
he wears a young man's crewcut.
no nonsense of bodily adornment,
a stand-up guy.

a lyrical one too
performing the more deliberate innovations
of the ballads--
"all the things you are,"
"my foolish heart"--
leaving the pyrotechnics
to the alto and soprano

of the young, dreadlocked antonio hart.

and an honest man:
after close to an hour-and-a-half,
he accepts applause with
"i won't pretend to you
that i was happy with that set.
i was not; 1 definitely was *not,*
and i will point no fingers
here in front of you,
but you may rest assured
that we will be much better
in the second set."

perhaps he feels that they have been sluggish,
nonchalant, before the sunday evening turnout,
the empty seats increased by strong desert winds
reaching into the seventies in miles per hour.
he's tried to get the sound man
to reduce the volume of his mike,
the jamming of the rhythm section
has been noticeably uninspired.
his protege has been perhaps a bit too cool
in wandering to and from the stage.
not to mention that donald harrison
has not even shown up.

at any rate, the next set is
a different story.

The Life Force Poems

ANDRE DERAIN: WINDOW AT VERS, 1912

for barbara voltmer

the narrow and elongate window,
frame within frame,
makes the outside world
a dead life of the living,
behind the still life of
plate, bowl, fruit, pitcher
on the dresser.

the vase of flowers on the windowsill,
a little to the right of center,
constitutes a fine transition
back and forth between
the wood of trees and that of furniture,
the growing and decaying all here
stopped in time,
shuttered in shadow,
draped in a brown study of
late afternoon/approach of night.

DAVID HOCKNEY: GARROWBY HILL, 1998

yes, art *can* exist in a vacuum.
it doesn't matter, for instance,
where this road comes from
or where it leads,
or why it's lavender.
the fields are plotted,

and the trees have been
planted in wind-breaking rows,
so certain inferences can be drawn
regarding the existence of human
ownership and agricultural employees,
but they ain't in evidence.

forget sociology.
forget culture.
forget the new or old
historicisms.

even the age of the artist
is absent.

after a century of subjectivity,
of perspective limited to consciousness,
a hundred years of human point-of-view,

it's refreshing to have
omniscience as an option.

EDWARD HOPPER: COMPARTMENT C, CAR 293, 1938

green is easy on the eyes.
so is she.
red hair goes well with
green; i bet her eyes are
green. her dress is navy blue,

as is her bell-shaped, slightly
floppy hat. she reads. we read
a lot in edward hopper.

The Life Force Poems

outside, white water flows
between brown banks beneath
a simple half-moon bridge.
a red sky disappears behind
the blackness.

we learn, in edward hopper, to
spend time alone. in edward
hopper we learn how to make
the time pass.

RICHARD DIEBENKORN: GIRL SMOKING

elegant legs, gracefully crossed.
not hopper's pallet, but
a diva on a divan,
knowing she's attractive,
but without illusions of divinity,
thus not a prima donna.

vulnerable shoulders.
a nipple out of nowhere.
she hugs herself, supports
an elbow on a forearm

anxiety as well as inhalation,
sophistication, but not
ellington exactly either.
the room an atmosphere of color
..and cologne?

home from the dance?

Gerald Locklin

home from the date?
home from the cabaret?

a lady in waiting.
wondering if he will show?

we used to be able to feel good
about the way we smoked,
the way we looked when smoking.
it was theatre.
a lot of women that i dated
used to smoke. after sex
a cigarette, a drink,
pleasure after pleasure,
sitting up in bed
or at a kitchen table.
killing time until the next time,
friendly conversations,
with each other, with ourselves.

they write me sometimes,
now married with grown children,
spacious homes and gardens,
justly proud and doting husbands.

good times, they say:
we had good times.

they <u>were</u> good times.

they say, i don't know if
you will remember me.

yes, yes, i do.
now more than ever,

The Life Force Poems

after thirty or more years
a sketch,
a smoky reverie of red coiffure
a femininity gone out of fashion.

yes, yes, they were the best times,
though perilous, now proved imperishable.

my god i'm glad that i have
women to remember
and that to some at least
i meant good times

TERI'S SOCK POEM

it was only a few months after
i was hospitalized two-and-a-half weeks
with bloodclots in the lungs
and on oxygen and out of work
for a number of weeks after that.
i was doing well now, but was still working
my way back towards some semblance of
self-confidence. it was the first party
i'd attempted to attend, an outdoor barbecue
at a graduate student's home,
with live music and dancing.

i had been quite the partier in my day
and now I was feeling pretty out of it,
cold sober and knowing my lungs
weren't ready for any dance floor.
i filled up my plate with potato salad
and found myself sitting next to

a petite young lady with dark hair who
turned out to be one of those rare
conversationalists who actually want to
hear whatever it is you have to say and
who exude warmth and sympathy. we talked
about my job, hers, people she had known
who had illnesses similar to mine.
the traveling each of us had done.
it turned out her boyfriend was in
one of my classes, a good guy, athletic,
ex-marine, now an m.a. candidate in literature,
someone i talked a lot of sports with.
i'd surmised anyway that she wasn't interested
in me in "that way," but she kidded with me,
almost flirted, and it was just close enough
to boy/girl talk to get me thinking maybe the
old days weren't entirely behind me, that
maybe i wasn't quite as over-the hill as
i'd walked in there feeling.
one of the things she teased me about
was the pair of black socks that i was wearing
with my birkenstocks. she said i needed
fuzzy socks, furry socks, something like that.

maybe i'm getting it all wrong:
it was three years ago.
I know i didn't mention that the black socks
were to cover a pair of jobst prescription
anti-embolism stockings.

anyway, when she found out that i wrote poems
she asked me if i was going to write one for
her, and I said, "sure,"
and she asked, "what will you write?"
and i said, "i'll write one about socks,"

The Life Force Poems

and she said, "no, you'll forget,"
and i said, "no, i won't - look i'm going
to jot a note to myself on this cocktail
napkin, and the next time i sit down to write
poems i won't be able to miss it."

and she seemed to get a real kick out of that.

but somehow i <u>did</u> manage to lose the napkin,
and every time i ran into her,
she'd ask about the sock poem
and each time i jotted another note
and folded it into my pocket,
and somehow these prompts always got mislaid,
which just never happens to my poem-ideas,
honest.

and now finally i'm sitting in a hotel
on the san francisco bay,
watching the planes land from the unusually
blue sky over the choppy, white-capped waters,
and at last I'm getting down on paper
what an exceptionally good heart teri has,
and what it meant to have such a lively and
attractive young lady pay me a little attention
at a very low point in my life,

and i know it wasn't uncharacteristic of her,
that she brightens people's lives every day,

and she and my former student,
who is now a colleague,
are still together,
and he'll probably give me a tough time
about having written this poem

just as he properly derides my annual boasts
that i'm about to take the floor
for the department intramural basketball team
and sky above the rim,

but i wish them all the best
as i pen this inadequate tribute to teri,
whose heart is as big as this bay,
as the blue sky above,

who listens to people,
and kids them about their socks,
and makes them feel good about themselves.

WINOLD REISS: HARLEM GIRL, 1925

she's been in my classes,
jet hair sculpted like that
of the daughter of a pharaoh.
gaze toward the future, though,
and neither naive nor implacable
in the face of what i stand for,
speak for.

neck and shoulders slender and
strong. breasts of a girl.
eyes of a woman,
features african and european
in proportion.

i'll lay it out for her
from socrates to the sonata,
cicero to sinatra,

The Life Force Poems

stonehenge/sissinghurst.
melanctha to *les miz,*
the magus to the wiz.
she'll take my teaching home with her.
let it sift and shift like sand,
pour it through an hourglass.
filter the impurities.

i'll never know if she'll decide
to give a rat's ass about rilke.

either way i'll go on liking her-
i've always had a weakness for *her* world,
from aesop to miles.
sugar ray to sugar ray.
ellison to baldwin,
muhammed ali to spike lee.

and i'm glad that she's still willing
to give my uncertain words attention.

JOHN JAMES AUDUBON: WHOOPING CRANE

look at me lift one foot.
i like to do that.
i like how long
every bit of us is.

i think i'll take
this lizard in my beak.
the brightly striped one.
i think i'll eat this one.
i left the plainer one for dead,

belly up,
and soft beneath the chin.

afterwards i'll have a sip
or two of the pond.
maybe a dip.
and aren't those leaves lovely?
i'm having a very nice day,
thank you,
another one.

VISHNU, SIEM REAP, 9TH CENTURY

a man needs many arms.
a god needs even more,
or none at all.

not from dust came we,
but water. we crawled
up on the land. we ruled
it without our knowledge. then
we thought to think about ourselves.

we had strong legs
to stand on, so we would

not fall off of the spinning
earth. our heads were pillars
also, to support the atmosphere
and sky. we mastered sleight -- of --
hand. we began to believe our
own magic.

The Life Force Poems

we had a tendency to go too far.

DAVID HOCKNEY:
THE ROAD TO YORK THROUGH SLEDMERE

i've walked the roads
into the heart of villages.
be sure to look both ways,
right and left, right and wrong,

before you cross the road. the
lorries have been lifted from
this scene. you are the lorry.
you're the man from mars,

the ancient astronaut, come
back to see how things have
fared. you trusted that your
deeds would last a while here

and they did. the oldest thing
is usually the churchyard, and
the living grow back centuries
as well. every village has its

war memorial. every village has
its color. this one's red as
oklahoma clay. high walls make
best neighbors. chimneys keep

us cozy. god is green. don't
speed on through to york. you'll
only find more walls there. virtual
medieval. markets where the markets

were. a lump of danish horseshit pet-
rified. pub lunch at club med(ieval).
medicinal (real) ale. stay a moment
for a parlor tea in sledmere. have

your pub lunch here, a shepherd's.
breathe blue smoke, the strong crust
of friendly breath. listen to syllables
wrestled up from roughened throats,

tasted, chewed, and gently spat
like turf. mud is an absolute.
stand still an afternoon here.
you'll probably be in a rush

to get home, next time through.

THE OLDEST INTERN IN AMERICA

the two young mothers at our table
are discussing the stage their kids
are at of "playing doctor."

it's been over fifty years
since i played doctor.

i gaze upon these comely women,
bright and slender,
and reflect it just might be time
for a refresher course.

The Life Force Poems

THE POET'S HELPMATE

writing a poem about a whistler beach scene,
i ask her, "give me the name of
a plant that grows at the beach."

"ice plant?" she says.

"no," i say, "i've already used ice plant,
how about something that grows on the
sand dunes of oregon."

"pampers grass," she says.

"pampas grass," i say: "that's good."
"no." she says, "<u>pampers</u> grass."

but i catch on in time that
she is trying to trick me into
making a fool out of myself by
publishing a deadly serious poem
about diapers.

LEAVING HOME

at the start of the fall semester
I find myself taking on way too much
more work than I know I should:

theses and directed studies students,

committees on and off campus,
the writing of prefaces, reviews,
letters of recommendation,
poetry readings,
moonlighting stints...

i wonder why i am being so foolhardy.

and then, waking in the middle of the night,
it comes to me that i have no doubt subconsciously
been trying to fill the enormous, incalculable void
that the departure of my daughter to begin college,
four hundred miles away,
is, after eighteen years,
leaving in my daily life
and in the depths of my being.

BLAST FROM THE PAST

bumping in the oakland
taxi to the motown station,
thirty years from 1964,
garfono's pizzeria jukebox,
"my girl," "my guy," the
righteous brothers, dancing in
the aisles, the march on
pershing square, lifted by two
marshalls from the federal
building, bailing friends
out, jazz at shelly's manne
hole, in love with love, the life
the blacks led, gazing down from
el sereno as watts burned, fired

The Life Force Poems

in the first year of teaching, all
the intensity of starting out, of
the origins, of when it all
began that took us through today
a changed man in a changed
land, moved again by music
that meant hope, sex, history,
intoxication, everything.

INCOMPLETE REFORMATION

when i used to be a big drinker,
especially in my beer-drinking days,
i was always pissing in embarrassing
and/or inappropriate places:
in closets, under doors, up onto
mantelpieces, and of course, jumping
out of cars to relieve myself next to the
fender or behind a tree.

when i quit drinking three years ago,
though, i figured those days of
lawless micturition were behind me.

friday night, however, driving to a
reading in l.a. and trapped in rush-
hour traffic for almost two hours,
i found my bladder near to bursting
by the time i got off the freeway in
beverly hills. there were still a
number of excruciating red lights and
left turns between me and the venue,
so i pulled off on an affluent- but-

darkened sidestreet, parked half-
blocking the driveway of an unlighted
house, positioned myself between the
passenger door and a big old tree, and
hastily unzipped. i'd only unstoppered
about ten percent of the pressure before
a pair of headlights made a turn onto the
lane. but even though i had to tighten
the sphincter instantly, tuck the thing
away, and return to the driver's side,
feigning a check of the tires for
flattening, that bit of depressurization
had made a world of difference, especially
when i left my seat belt off. i was able
to make it to the county museum of art
without drenching my pants.

the beverly hills police would have loved
to nail a bearded poet/professor from
long beach for that public nuisancing:
have you seen the film <u>down and out in
beverly hills?</u> this was not the sort of
behavior i should have been indulging in,
given my new regime of respectability,
even if i had replaced the pitchers of
budweiser with liters of caffeine-free diet
pepsi. still i know that, in his hillside palos
verdes grave, charles bukowski must have chuckled.

CÉZANNE: SELF-PORTRAIT, 1878-80

he looked like a russian,
like each of the karamazovs.

The Life Force Poems

he looked like my late editor,
marvin malone, another man of the prairies
who contemplated mountains.

after god grew bored with us,
the artist had to be
priest, intellectual, and sensualist,
progenitor and pathologist,
doctor and patient,
architect, mathematician, physicist,
marxist, freudian, darwinian,
and skeptic of it all.
he had to see himself
as others saw him
and as no one else did,
had to empathize with his enemies
while anticipating their gambits.
he had to be she,
and she, he.
he had to dream without sleeping.

he had, in other words, to know everything,
and learn how not to think.

this was the job description;
many did not qualify.

oh, incidentally, he also had to be
born to the task:
there were no A's for effort.

Gerald Locklin

LEE KRASNER

when are they going to
stop asking us to accept
the wives of the giants -
in this case jackson pollock-
as the creative or intellectual
equals of their spouses,
overshadowed only because of
the "oppression" of their gender.
picasso, einstein, hemingway, fitzgerald,
all of their mates enjoyed
a feminist-promoted vogue
and then receded to, at best,
supporting roles,
at worst, jealous antagonism.

The catalogue (for the l.a. county
exhibit) says krasner "frequently
made reference to other artists,"
with her <u>palingenesis</u> a homage to
matisse and stella. it strikes me as
mere uninspired imitation,
dull and formulaic,
lifeless and unbeautiful.

we're told <u>bald eagle</u> derives
from depression-era frugality,
the female tradition of quilting,
and that the self is formed
"through an ongoing discourse with others."
the first two are mildly interesting ideas,

The Life Force Poems

the third a postmodernist cliche and half-truth.
when all is said and done,
who wants to look at it?

it's also termed a compensation for
"her husband's inadequacies
occasioned by advancing alcoholism."
her work, however, is not adequate
to blaze forth with the parallel
complexities and lightning of
the molecule and microcosm.

prophesy is second-hand
and second-rate picasso.

her <u>self-portrait</u> (1930)
is more interesting
i can sense what pollock saw in her,
the slightness of her arms and shoulders,
vulnerability of breasts,
but he should have been forewarned
by the aggressive fullness of those lips,
the resentments simmering already in those eyes.

i see one sick puppy.

he was a genius;
she was not.
and genius may be simply, largely,
in the genes,
though cultured in the crucible
of childhood, social contexts.
he had it; she did not.
gertrude stein did; alice didn't.
virginia woolf did; leonard was a plodder.

it isn't fair; it ain't nice.
no doubt it is "mean spirited" of me
to point it out.

but it's the simple truth
and i am sick of being asked
to diplomatically swallow lies.

JAN VAN HUYSEM: BOUQUET OF FLOWERS IN AN URN

i couldn't begin to identify
this linnean multiplicity of blossoms
(i think i spot cornflowers, angels' breath).

there aren't this many crayons
in my deluxe carton.

i'd need a dictionary to
describe the plenitude of
shapes (more various than sea
lifes, the essence of
organic profligacy)

and i years ago tossed my
thesaurus out the window.

some days
(some years, some decades)
an artist just wants to show off

(and, accidentally, he celebrates
creation).

The Life Force Poems

AELBERT CUYP: THE FLIGHT INTO EGYPT

it doesn't matter that the terrain
is not that of the gaza
but of italy, wooded paths, eroded cliffs,
postcard clouds,
fresher water.

it doesn't matter that it
isn't even italy, a country that
the artist never visited.

it doesn't matter that the
garb is high dutch,
the path well worn and paradisal,
and joseph an erasmus.

what matters is drumbeats:

the orchestration of the lacy,
sharp, and curvilinear,
delineation of rhythm section
synchronized for luminosity,
a melody that ranges from
the pale blue mist of morning
to finessing of the facial mysteries.

SIMON DE VLIEGER: VIEW OF A BEACH

the many-masted, canvas-bosomed warships

and the sleeker clippers
sit upon the waters,
having come or soon to go.
a man and woman kiss, maturely,
welcome or farewell.
man with a spyglass; a lion; a
dog stretched out like a lion
wives and merchants dressed for the weather
in leather and looseness,
leggings and boots,
horsecarts and hawsers:
the daily commerce of the guiltless.
getters and spenders.

when the sea is as flat as the land,
you learn to make do with an endless sky.
where the water's cold,
you take clouds for granted.
in rotterdam the ships are fashioned
of timbers money never grew on anyway.

thus, commerce is a constant.

a thriving people,
practical and realistic,
paid its artists handsomely
(though less than royalty)
to hold the mirror of the beautiful
up to the mirror of production.

JACOB VAN RUISDAEL: THE GREAT OAK

it occupies the three-foot canvas

The Life Force Poems

fills the center
blocks the sun,
ignores the clouds,
mocks the foregrounding of
our agitated and homunculus
transactions

gives green to everything
that grows beneath it.

travelling through time and space
like gulliver,
richard milhaus nixon,
that noted cultural appraiser
would have said,
"that is a great oak".

GO WITH THE FLOW
(AND END UP WHERE MOST FLOWS DO)

i'm reading this review of
an l.a. production of ionesco's *rhinoceros*
in a supposedly radical weekly,
and to my gradual astonishment
i begin to realize that the reviewer
considers the guy who sees everyone else
turning into rhinoceroses
to be the fool of the play,
the butt of the satire.
he figures this reactionary
is either paranoid or stubbornly
unable to adapt.
this social misfit isn't aware of

what a laughable, capitalistic, patriarchal thing
the postmodern theorists have 'proved'
individualism to be,
not to mention that,
the unitary self being an illusion anyway,
one might as well just mix one's
mental molecules into the great
collectivist, collaborationist stew.

my first reaction is, "jesus christ,
indeterminate interpretations were never
intended to be quite <u>this</u> indeterminate,
were they?"

but on second thought, i have to shake
my head in admiration - what an editorial
brainstorm: to have *rhinoceros*
reviewed by a rhinoceros.

HAIR OF THE DOG

i have obtained from my dog's vet
a prescription for tranquilizers
which i only use, judiciously,
when thunderstorms or holiday fireworks
threaten to drive the poor thing
right through the plate-glass doors
that separate her ample yard
from our cat-crowded living room.

but i hate to do it even then
because in the morning she looks
so depressed and bedraggled and

practically cross-eyed with fatigue.
i realize that i am looking at
the face of a labrador retriever
with a hangover.

and the sad and funny thing is that
i know there were innumerable times
just a few years ago
when i looked and felt
even worse.

MAYBE IT'S THE DIFFERENCE BETWEEN BEING AN INTELLECTUAL AND SIMPLY BEING INTELLIGENT

whenever everyone agrees on an idea,
whether to the "left" or "right,"
you can be sure that it is
not so much a *wrong* idea
as not really an *idea* at all,
but just a verbalization designed to
substitute itself for a thought,
for the process of thinking:

thus, one says, "all life is sacred,"
the other, "a woman's body is her own,"
and yet another, "everything's
subjective anyway."

half-way through her first psychology
class my daughter asked me,

"why isn't it obvious to these theoreticians
that behavior is not the product

of nature or of nurture
but of both,
and maybe of something not-yet-named as well,
and maybe not really even a product?"

"i don't know,"
i said;
"i really don't know why
it isn't obvious to them."

WHAT I LIKE ABOUT INSPECTOR MORSE

i like inspector morse
because of the things he likes:

the latin language and literature,
the english language and literature,
women,
real english ale,
football,
loyalty,
his job,
oxford.

i like inspector morse because of
the things he cannot stand:

the disloyal,
predators,
the social sciences,
self-important academics.

then there's wagner:

The Life Force Poems

i like inspector morse because
he's not afraid to like wagner,
who was not a saint.
inspector morse does not confuse
wagner's music with his politics.
inspector morse does not presume
to judge, does not waste his precious
time judging, a man who lived in a
time in which we are not ourselves
living. if he is going to judge anything,
it will be his own era,
his contemporaries,
himself,

and for relaxation and inspiration
he will enjoy the harmonies and dynamics
of a musical genius, one who did,
incidentally, understand the relationship
of love to death,
romantic love, the loss of loved ones,
ancient familial bonds,
the love of power,
the love of wealth,
the love of self,
possessive love,
obsessive love,
and the relationship of
all the forms of love
to murder.

AUGUSTE RODIN:
SEVERED HEAD OF JOHN THE BAPTIST, MARBLE

well, if they have their hearts set
on cutting something off (and you
can be absolutely sure they do), it's
just as well the head go first. i
mean, would you rather keep your head,
while they cut everything else off
first? that was pretty much the theory
behind the art of drawing and quartering,
which did so much to define the age of
shakespeare as the most truly and
unabashedly human of the ages. also,
better that your head end up a marble
than start out that way. anyway, rodin
tried to give it to the queen of belgium,
but the great war was in progress (not
so great if you were in it) and it never
got to her. what a shame: what woman
wouldn't appreciate a memento of sweet
salome, patroness of the scorned,
the sublimely sublimated?

JAMES ABBOTT McNEILL WHISTLER:
SYMPHONY IN WHITE, NO. 3

the women lounge about now, bored.
how to pass the day?

perhaps they'll take some pleasure

The Life Force Poems

from each other.
who could blame them?
or do they dream of men?

i doubt it.

the fan has dropped to the floor,
the flowers droop, unpollenated.

JAMES ABBOTT McNEILL WHISTLER: SYMPHONY IN WHITE, NO. 2: THE LITTLE WHITE GIRL

the little girl is not so little anymore.
she asks her mirror who she is,
and who she will be.

the self she sees has aged and dulled.

springflowers bloom.
her fan is from the orient.

her girlhood must die to
give birth to us.

NO OFFENSE INTENDED

Sorry, but if i awoke one morning
with a vagina
i would stick my dick in it.

or

i would go back to sleep
and try again later.

or

i would get dressed very quickly.
(actually, i would probably kill myself.)

THE WORDS

it's amazing how few young poets
think it's important to expand
their vocabularies and the rhetorical range
of their sentences and paragraphs.
they think that writing is
experiences and emotions,
not words.
and yet you don't write
experiences and emotions;
you express your experiences and emotions
in words.
i tell them to take a year of latin or french.
i tell them to buy one of those paperbacks
that tell you how to increase your word
power.
i tell them to get a more articulate
circle of friends.

i tell them how i watched ron koertge
turn an excellent vocabulary
into an immense one,
copying down the words he didn't know,
looking them up in the dictionary,

The Life Force Poems

taping them to the wall,
making a point of using them
in his conversation and writing
until they became second nature to him.

only a few of the young people are listening.

it's more fun to go in search of experiences,
especially the easy and pleasurable ones.

but the ones who are paying attention
are the ones whose words we'll be reading
after the others have quit writing,

because if literature
were just experiences and emotions,
not words and their arrangements,
every guy in the bar
would have been bukowski.

PIERRE BONNARD: SELF-PORTRAIT

"at his toilet."
what an ugly concept.
less so in french, i suppose.
but what a humiliating waste of time.
preparing to meet the world.
amending appearance.
fussing over facial hair.
having to look at ourselves in the mirror.
making ourselves smell like flowers,
or the pancreatic archipelago of whales.

i get up, wash my face, and

Gerald Locklin

brush my teeth. pull myself back
into yesterday's jeans and tee-shirt.
haven't shaved since 1964.
take my pills with diet coke.
give the dog a biscuit,
get the paper from the sidewalk,
settle into my chair for a couple
of hours of work.

the closest i come to human contact
is the occasional phone call.
i smell good enough for the cats;
i smell better than the dog.

around noon i'll shower and swim
at the y. put on clean clothes.
weigh myself on the way out.
go eat spaghetti with artichokes and
mushrooms, a salad, garlic bread,
more diet coke. off to classes.

maybe bonnard enjoyed freshening up,
but he doesn't look particularly thrilled.
even artists should avoid mirrors, pierre.
look how they fucked up lacan.
there's no improving on arnulfi's wedding
anyway. i hope i'm never caught dead
at my toilet, especially literally.

**THE MOST THREADBARE CLICHE IN
THE MARRIAGE BUSINESS**

he'd been working his ass off when,
out of nowhere, she said,

The Life Force Poems

"you're no fun anymore."
what did that mean?
that be was more fun when he used to
stay out till dawn?
that he was no fun now that he'd started
taking her to art museums and operas
instead of limiting his cultural interests
to sports?
that he was no fun because
he took the responsibility for the taxes,
and getting the kids' college applications in,
and making and canceling the family doctors' appointments,
and dealing with insurance
companies and repair men?
maybe it was because he wouldn't pretend
to find stimulating idiotic programs
like <u>the x files</u>.

no. he knew what it was.
it was just that she could no longer
find anything else about him
to criticize.

GUSTAVE CAILLEBOTTE: FLOOR-SCRAPERS, 1875

like sprinters in their starting blocks.
like rowers about to churn backwards.

no, like galley slaves.

the rightward diagonal of the floorboards
against the vanishing point to the left
of the light.

Gerald Locklin

what is stripped away is not only
the shavings of wood. and yet, the
musculature of the manual laborer: he
does not require a lifetime membership
at the local health club. but
he will not live long.

a wine bottle by the wall:
vin ordinaire. the zinc bar on
the way home. we call it "miller time."

the dignity of labor?
we were taught by the nuns and priests
that all honest work was noble,
and it might as well be, if
there's no way out of it. ironically, our
irish families sent us to their schools
so that we'd rise above the jobs they
had to do, and we did. but we
drank also, our thirst no less than that
of these hard workers, working their
fingers, as the phrasing had it, to
the bone. we drank every night for thirty years,
and we outlived them, but not much longer.

a room, a world, of brown, beige, sepia,
of grays and glaze and glare,
of dross not gold.

an ornamental grating,
like a tarnished, jewel-less tiara.

what does it add up to?
anything?

The Life Force Poems

GUSTAVE CAILLEBOTTE:
PARIS STREET: RAINY DAY, 1977

what would walt whitman have made
of paris, the opposition of the cobblestones
and balustrades, the apparition of
umbrellas and the concave skydome?
eyes to the right, our destinies are
at left angles to our dreams. eyes
to the pavement, everywhere but at
each other. commerce is a wedge the
width of a city block, and *le printemps*
is a department store. we dress in top
hat, vest, and a bowtie for no reason except
that we've told each other that we must.
and yet six years later, blood stained
these streets, the paris commune, civil
war, the humiliation of the franco-prussian.
now the bourgeoisie as usual, and black
is never out of fashion. along the
boulevards of haussmann one finds neither
heaven nor the blues, no broken dreams,
no dreams at all. still, the precipitation
lends a pleasant sheen to them, though magritte
slouches towards the suburbs to be born.

CHAIM SOUTINE: HANGING TURKEY AND HEAD AND CARCASS OF A HORSE

turn studio to slaughterhouse.
let the blood drip from

the bodies of the birds and animals.
smear the carcasses with extra blood,
if necessary. slash the skins:
allow the parasites their infestation;
give praise to putrefaction.
the ripe will soon be rancid.
we are talking rot and stink.
no pretty fictions of the spirit.

put our pets in their places.
personally butcher them.
remind them they are meat.

ED RUSCHA:
HOLLYWOOD,1968

the hollywood sign on the horizon.
sunset behind the hollywood hills.
a sky at the infra-red end
of the cinematic spectrum.
the oblong dimensions of cinemascope,
even the illusion of depth
from the gradual foregrounding
of the latter letters.

you hear the hollywood bowl.
you sense the spirit of james dean.
mullholland murders and machinations
flicker in the noir beyond the frame,
the roar of road-rage
though the cahuenga pass,
you see why they named that crosstown artery
sunset boulevard.

The Life Force Poems

but all of l.a. is excluded, wisely,
save this marriage of
man the maker and mother nature.

DIRTY OLD MEN AND THE NEW DOUBLE STANDARD

bukowski was right to
apply the term to himself
before anyone else could.
he always had a knack for
launching pre-emptive strikes,
although they were sometimes unnecessary,
even downright paranoid.
but i'm sure he would have been accused
by the envious
of being a dirty old man
if he hadn't already blithely applied
the label to himself.

the problem is i've never understood
what is supposed to be dirty:
is being old dirty?
is being old and sexual dirty?
is being old and sexual and finding
the young attractive dirty?
would it be okay for us to call
a mature woman
who was sexual with a much younger man
a dirty old woman?
an old slut?

or would we be expected to treat her
as some sort of heroic model
of female self-realization?

maybe the dirty old women
don't want to compete with younger women
for the attentions
of the dirty old men.

ARE THE SOCIAL POLICE MISREPRESENTING THEIR CONSTITUENCY?

in spite of the current reign of terror,
i still compliment women on their appearances:
a colorful new outfit,
a fresh hairdo,
a tan,
a little weight loss (although this
one can be risky).

it seems the natural thing to do,
the friendly thing,
and i don't follow up
with an invitation to lunch.

i sometimes wonder if
it will get me in hot water, but,
so far, no woman has seemed anything other than
quite visibly pleased to be complimented
on her comely appearance.

EDWARD HOPPER: CAPE COD EVENING, 1938

i thought i was the only one
who never mowed his lawn?

The Life Force Poems

whoever heard of wheat for a lawn?
buffalo grass east of beantown?
a forest floor of waving grain?

a man's summer house is his
castle. a stoop for a
throne? a corinthian pseudo-
portico? the collie without a collar
will not look at, let alone come to,
the king in his v-necked undershirt.
even the dog is shaggy. the woman
is dowdy, stout from head to toe,
busty, bellied, big-legged,
determined. her hair and his
are as rusty as the dog's.

maybe they are the servants, yes,
or the caretakers. yes, that would
account for his biceps. and this,
the <u>back</u> door -- thus, no walkway.
that's why they seem so working
class, unjeweled, dully attired,
out of place here, stolid, acting
like recent immigrants, perhaps
from ireland or scandinavia.
blue trees?
blue moon?
blue setting sun?
a blue overcoat and
thus no real shadows?

the remains of the day.
when you come to the end
of a day as perfectly uneventful
as yesterday and tomorrow. one

day closer to night. night and
day, you are the no one. and
worst of all, you still have
each other.

RAILWAY STATION

it arched above us
like the paris opera,
but the sky was
its chagall. we were
perpetual rubberneckers never
taking the metropolis entirely
for granted, always hoping that
our work here would be leavened
with free play, free thought,
a world of spaciousness
sufficient to ourselves and generations
that would pour forth from us.
we could go forth from here.
we could return.
we could find all that an interval required
here, from steam-baths to a box of
barricinis, toiletries to philosophic
tomes. the steel itself was music,
and the crowds a cinema. light
came and light went forth. production
and consumption were the same here.
purveyors and consumers were the same.
labor became capital.
the center held.
the base was built to last,
the superstructure to evolve, the

The Life Force Poems

infrastructure an extension of our
hearts, minds, guts. we came, we
saw, we conquered and were conquered
by our conjurings.

we have not gone away.
we come and go.
we mingle; we abide;
we fear, but we continue,
only wondering if maybe now
there are too many of us.
maybe not enough,
maybe we've run out of undiscovered
caverns where our dreams were once
enacted.

THE HOUSEHOLD GODS HE'S ALLOWED

two frames hang above his work desk,
put there by his wife.
one contains the cover of <u>life</u> magazine
for september 1, 1952,
with the penetrating gaze of his god,
ernest hemingway, whose <u>old man and the sea</u>
was published in that issue.
(it sold, incidentally, for 20 cents.)

this dates from before their marriage,
from a time when she still loved him
and hadn't learned to hate his writing.

the other is a collage of photos
and commemorative stamps of babe ruth.

she chose it over one of lou gehrig.
it was a nice gesture in a way because
she knew he'd always been a rabid yankees' fan,
but she also knew he'd always mainly wanted
to put up a poster of mickey mantle,
his childhood hero,
whereas the babe was really before his time.
he figures it wasn't so much that she objected
to the mick's notorious boozing and womanizing-
somewhat akin to his own-
after all, the bambino was just as bad-
so much as that she wished to make
a conciliatory offering while still asserting
her ultimate control over the domestic premises.

he doesn't mind very much
papa and the bronx bomber-
what a fine pair of spiritual overseers.
he's written some pretty good stuff
with the two of them peering down
on his writing pads.

thank god she didn't opt for
the saintly, early-thwarted iron man.

THE NEW HISTORICISM

in the lobby of the musical theatre,
he beckons to his daughter,
now a college girl: "i have something
that i want to show you."

on the wall are framed the posters and

The Life Force Poems

stills from *dreamgirls,* the first musical
he ever took her to. she was only four,
just barely old enough to be admitted.
he took her by himself, picked a middle
aged woman who looked trustworthy to
keep an eye on her in the ladies' room.
they sat in the back row, where she could
stand on the seat if she wanted and direct
the orchestra, and he rationed candy to her.

she says she doesn't remember it,
and her mother,
who claims to hate liars,
says, "i wasn't invited,"

this woman who for fifteen years
wouldn't go anywhere with him, out
of spite, without the buffer of the children.
"of course you were," he says,
and she decides to drop it,
perhaps beginning to realize that,
for the rest of her life,
it may be him or no one.

AT THE ABSTRACT EXHIBITION

if i were an art teacher
i think i would urge my art students,
as i do my poetry students,
to give every art work a title.
i simply notice that these abstract paintings
that have titles seem more focused
emotionally, intellectually, technically,

or in some other way
than those that don't.

maybe "untitled" in other words,
actually means "unfinished."

and please don't tell me how
a true work of art
remains always in process,
and that no art work is ever truly finished.

this one is.

DAVID HOCKNEY: THE ROAD ACROSS THE WOLDS

england is a field of fields.
hedges create fields.
hedges vary with the shires,
from rock to sod to thicket.

yorkshire's wolds are the top
of yorkshire's world. yorkshire
rolls across its wolds. you
wind the road across the worlds.

at the top of the world
a house stands firm in the midst
of the rolling fields. crops
color the fields, birth to burn.

today the seasons stand side by side.
woods break the wind.
space travels; time stands stolen.

The Life Force Poems

sea, air, and salt are one.
you are everywhere at once.

ANOMIE

as many times as i looked it up,
i could never remember what it meant,
even though i should have been able
to conceptualize it as
the etymological opposite of *bonhomie*.

i think the concept was just too alien
to me, i was too passionate about so
many things, all those things about
which the young of my generation found
it easy to emote:

social justice;
sex, alcohol, sports, friends;
culture (pop and with a capital C);
competing;
writing;
our children.

now, a bit older, i still feel strongly
about many of the above,

but i do find it,
as time goes by,
a lot easier to remember
the definition of *anomie*.

Gerald Locklin

I'M FILING THIS TECHNIQUE AWAY FOR A RAINY DAY

when we pass a house with a particularly
vicious watchdog snarling through a gate-
a doberman or pit-bull, for example-
my loving chocolate lab keeps its eyes
straight ahead, shies a bit towards me,
and trots to the farthest diagonal of
the threatening canine's fiefdom where
it pauses long enough to mark the grass
with pee.

no matter how many bully-dogs we pass
on any given stroll,
the reservoir never seems to run dry.

JEAN ANTOINE WATTEAU: L'ACCORD PARFAIT

perfect accord? perfect harmony?
as the museum mag points out
this has to be high irony,
a satire of the pastoral tradition.
the flutist playing from a score
held for him by a maiden
has a face that would be the envy
of lon chaney's wolf-man.
he has more scar tissue closing his eyes
that the relentless welterweight,
carmen basilio (the pride of the
canastota onion fields).

The Life Force Poems

his hands are as hirsute as moss
and he has to be as old as
the black forest itself.
it would take a trash-talk champion of
yo'-mama and the ugly stick
to do true insult justice to this guy.
i bet he knows the tune by heart
and is actually stealing glances
down her décolletage.

reclining at her feet,
mezzetin, the musical trickster,
is, i can tell
(perhaps because i would be)
giving serious thought to letting a hand
creep up under her skirts.

not that she's any starlet.
i wouldn't call her pretty, exactly,
and i suspect she's seen better days
than she's admitting to. her hair's
somewhat coarse, and i wouldn't bet
my last billion lira on her virginity.
come to think of it,
maybe they <u>are</u> a perfect match.
not beauty and the beast,
but pan and the soon-to-be-beastly.

behind them a courtier listens intently
to a woman with a comely, creamy
neck and shoulders. of course, we are
only seeing her from behind.
and men have always had to feign interest
in the things that interest women,
if they hope to get laid.

Gerald Locklin

GOD'S MASTERPIECES

one of the fringe benefits
of swimming laps at the ymca
is being in the presence
for a number of hours every week
of lifeguards as beautiful and various
as any young women anywhere in the world.
but, as with all things,
one grows used to their ambiance;
we come to take this exceptional privilege
for granted. perhaps it's like that for
people living in the yosemite valley.
their beauty is still operating on
our sense of well being,
but we are as unconscious of it
as of the sun in the sky, the
stately pines and palm trees.

what is even more remarkable, however,
is that they are so unaware
of their own physical perfection
that they seem oblivious to
our imperfections also,
our flab and veins and wrinkles
and discolorations. i've never even
caught one of them looking at
any of us with distaste, let alone
saying anything that might bum us out.

so i swim on in the presence of
these wonders of the natural and human worlds
unselfconscious of my body

The Life Force Poems

for perhaps the first time in my life.

AND WHO KNOWS WHAT
GOES ON IN THOSE PLACES?

at a party for a young artist
i walk into a kitchen thick with
smoke of cannabis and quip,

"kind of a strong bouquet in here--
what is it, garlic?

a young poet follows me back to
the other room and asks,

"i know you don't approve of drugs,
but that didn't upset you, did it?"

jesus, i think, i know i lead
a pretty healthy lifestyle nowadays,
and my hair may be thinning a bit,
but do these kids think i spent
the last forty years in a monastery?

FERNAND LEGER: LEISURE, HOMAGE TO DAVID, 1948-49

such hearty men,
such robust, big-limbed women--only
in france would they envision wearing
three-piece suits in the marxist paradise.

Gerald Locklin

a bicycle in every millennial garage.
congratulatory peace-doves in the puffy clouds.
a sky as monochromatic blue
as the uniform smile plastered on
the comrade's faces.
tires growing on trees.

how did humanity ever fall for
the communist utopia? nobility of
soul, or just plain naivete? i
suppose it was the old seduction of
not wanting to seem less altruistic
than the rest of the intellectuals-
liberal morality substituting for
socioeconomic analysis. also, the
collective as a cure for loneliness.

okay, there was a dream--that we could
be better people than we'd ever been.
only the institutions of society
were holding us back. we thought that
maybe we could trust each other.

and yet this was to be accomplished by
the cynicism of ends justifying means.

we should have known we couldn't
really stand each other,
not for very long at least,
and surely not *en masse*.

The Life Force Poems

MARVIN MALONE
(WHO KNEW A POEM WHEN HE SAW ONE)

what he had:

business sense. a sense of responsibility. pride without ego sickness. both sides of the brain. the empiricism of the scientist. the rage of the just. virility. sticktoitiveness. willpower. self-confidence (no need for committees). the courage to say no. the courage to say yes to what he knew would outrage. a tolerance of artistic vanity, self-doubt, bravado, bad faith, addiction, delusion, mendacity. a willingness to listen, to forgive and forget, to afford second chances. the capacity to keep confidences confidential. wisdom to impart to others, though who can ever claim it for himself?

good game plan that he did not abandon.

love of what he was doing.
the belief that what he was doing was worthwhile.

what he gave:

port in the literary storm.
a forum for the poetry of the people.
an armor against elitism.
a community.
permission, validation, reinforcement, all those good things that
    the educational psychologists belatedly find names for.
sometimes instruction.
often a renewal of strength, of determination.
the possibility of permanence, that our words might be preserved.
hope.

what he left us:

the opportunity and obligation to stand on our own two feet.
the hunch (which would appall him) that somehow he still
    knows what we're up to.

when he comes to mind:

often, but most commonly when i'm typing up my poems for
submission and i smile, "here's one that he would have liked,"
and frown, "i wonder if there's anyone else out there who will."
and then, as he would want, i put it in the mail.

HAPPINESS

so many people search for it.
this search for personal happiness
becomes all their lives are about.

i was raised to think in terms of
accomplishments, for oneself or
for others, of goals, of striving.

　　rest was something for the next
life
　　peace was something put off till
eternity.
　　happiness was a static thing to
want,
　　an artificial and impossible par-
adise.
　　better to keep on trying to accom-
plish

The Life Force Poems

    what one has set out to accom-
plish
        in one's life.

        and yet, without seeking it,
        and even now that i've quit booze,
        or maybe especially now that i i've
quit booze,
        i often find that, momentarily at
least,
        i am extremely happy, even quiet-
ly ecstatic.

        and sure i get "stressed out," espe-
cially
        when i take on or have thrust
upon me,
        more than time realistically
allows,

        but something tells me that,
        in spite of struggle, strife, and
tension,

        and regardless of what the future
brings,

        i have known, on balance, much
more happiness
        than those who go through life
thinking
        that it's playing hide-and-seek
with them.

Gerald Locklin has published over eighty volumes of poetry, fiction, and literary essays including Charles Bukowski: A Sure Bet, Go West Young Toad, *and* Candy Bars: Selected Stories *(Water Row Press). Charles Bukowski called him "One of the great undiscovered talents of our time." The Oxford Companion to Twentieth Century Literature in the English Language calls him "a central figure in the vitality of Los Angeles writing." His works have been widely translated and he has given countless readings here and in England. He teaches at California State University, Long Beach.*